Deciphering Leadership

The Emerging Leaders' Guide to Navigating Power + Politics, Gaining Influence and Achieving Sustainable Success

Heather Connery

Deciphering Leadership:
The Emerging Leaders' Guide to Navigating Power + Politics,
Gaining Influence and Achieving Sustainable Success
© 2025 Heather Connery

ISBN: 9781919209906 Paperback

Published by: Inspired By Publishing

The strategies in this book are presented primarily for enjoyment and educational purposes. Every effort has been made to trace copyright holders and obtain their permission for the use of copyright material.

The information and resources provided in this book are based upon the authors' personal experiences. Any outcome, income statements or other results, are based on the authors' experiences and there is no guarantee that your experience will be the same. There is an inherent risk in any business enterprise or activity and there is no guarantee that you will have similar results as the author as a result of reading this book.

The author reserves the right to make changes and assumes no responsibility or liability whatsoever on behalf of any purchaser or reader of these materials.

Deciphering Leadership:
How Successful Leaders Lead to Navigate Power Dynamics
& Gaining Influence and Achieving Sustainable Success
© 2025 Heather Canady

Acknowledgements

Firstly, I would like to thank my husband and children for their support while I wrote this book and other research pieces of work.

The concept of Real Model originated from the awe-inspiring Leon Marseglia, CEO of the amazing company, The Youth Group. It made such a lasting impression on me that it has stuck with me for years. I witnessed good leaders on occasion make small mistakes, and then were vilified for years. They were being punished for a moment of humanness. But they were excellent Real Models. At the other end of the scale were the False Gods, which I think we have seen play out in real life, from overzealous managers to some industry and world leaders.

A huge thank you goes to all those who donated their time to this work. Thank you for sharing your experiences, being so open and honest on the highs and lows and everything in between on your leadership journey.

It would therefore be remiss if I didn't thank Real Models, previous managers, leaders (including some False Gods), mentors, coaches and sponsors who have given me the benefit of their wisdom over the years, or at least a good anecdote that I can use to help others.

Contents

Introduction

About This Book

"On our planet, leadership is arguably the most influential mechanism to shape societal activity for good or bad."
– Unknown

Yes, this is another leadership book, so why read this one?

This book is a companion for those who are entering emerging leadership, are already in it, or are reaching the destination of being fully emerged. It explores the journey, its trials and tribulations, and helps an emerging leader become a high-performing leader without losing their soul. I also aim to give the emerging leader an unfair advantage over others by laying out common pitfalls, how to spot them, avoid them, or navigate out of them.

Jeffrey Pfeffer, in his insightful and proactive book *Leadership BS,* said, "If we want to change the world of work and leadership conduct … we need to act on what we know rather than what we wish and hope for."[1] I couldn't agree more. This book is unvarnished and attempts to get to the heart of current challenges emerging leaders are facing, or will face, without indulging in toxic positivity.

This book isn't a traditional leadership book as it attempts to cross-fertilise a broader mix of academic theory from a mixture of social sciences, pop culture reflections, and the experience of leaders (the leadership participant group) throughout their leadership journey, brought together by a leader, but without me pontificating at length about my own journey. Instead, I have sought the wisdom of nearly forty leaders to share the good, the bad and the ugly of leadership. The leadership participant group, comprising almost forty individuals, ranged from students to Non-Executive Directors (NEDs), academics, industry figures and those recognised within the British honours system for their contributions to society.

"A traditional definition of leadership will not be debated as there are so many different definitions of leadership"[2], and for the purposes of the book, will rely on the Cambridge dictionary definition with one small amendment:

"A person who manages, controls, or influences other people, especially because of his or her ability to do so." The inclusion being influence, which reflects today's societal dynamic, e.g. thought leader, journalist, influencer, etc.

Leadership does not inherently equate to goodness or morality. A bad person (defined by unethical behaviour, exploitation or disregard for others) can still be a leader if they possess characteristics like charisma, strategic thinking or the ability to instil fear, and such leaders can achieve success in the short term through manipulative or authoritarian tactics. Whilst leadership is nuanced and complex (which the book goes into), at its simplest, there are universal good and bad traits. As with most definitions in the book, I rely heavily on standard definitions, and where I seek to redefine something new or different, I make that explicit..

Conversely, good leaders, often characterised by compassion, fairness and respect for others, may be perceived as weak if they fail to balance these characteristics with decisiveness and resilience.

This book is about the leadership journey and how to become a True Leader as opposed to an idealised, unrealistic model. Additionally, it issues a warning about False Gods or Goddesses (and may serve as a guide to prevent misguided Real Models from developing into False Gods). The use of the term "God" implies the masculine gender; in this context, it is merely using a generic term. No connotations of gender should be assumed in the context of this book; it could equally refer to Goddess or other genders.

LinkedIn is the platform for professionals, leaders, etc., a workplace Facebook, if you will. Like most social media it veers towards the positives, praise and recognition, awards being received in beautiful gowns and expensive suits, product launches celebrated with the cultural rituals of an industry (e.g. champagne in the legal sector), inspiring thought leadership quotes, hard-fought-for money to support charity work making the world a better place for all and some crossing finish lines or standing on mountains – but this is just a snapshot of the positive realities of leadership.

As Jeff Bezos points out, "When somebody congratulates Amazon on a good quarter...I say thank you. But what I'm thinking to myself is... those quarterly results were pretty much fully baked about three years ago."[3] This can be translated into the above examples. A leader didn't just decide to scale a mountain and climb it the next day; preparation and training would have been undertaken over a period involving grit and discipline. Products can take years to develop, and recognition can take months or years of hard work.

Rather than exploring the LinkedIn leadership profile, this book is about the journey to train for a mountain climb, the fortitude to develop a product after multiple failed iterations, and the resilience to work long hours and persevere in grafting and toiling to build something that may or may not receive recognition. Much of a leader's day-to-day work involves navigating difficult decisions, managing conflicts, and facing uncertainties, while motivating others toward shared goals. Recognising and embracing this duality is essential for sustainable leadership. Meta-analysis suggests that at an executive at board level, time is spent navigating a series of challenges (95% to 97%), versus hours spent focusing on the good or great elements of leadership (5% to 3%). It is the former that this book spends most of its time on – this is the content that is not on social media.

The chapter's opening quote is not just provocative; it is a reality. A glance at global news reveals the multitude of challenges humanity faces, and has holistically faced in some shape or form, as it has always done. While not all these challenges are caused by leaders, it is leadership that determines how they are addressed and ultimately ended. This book will also address the quiet truths that are often not spoken of, examining the moral weight of leadership within the above external context, while exploring the internal identity shifts leaders undergo.

In the late 1980's the U.S. Army War College developed a framework called VUCA, which stands for volatile, uncertain, complex and ambiguous. It was a decade later that it started to be applied in the business world.[4] Essentially, the world is characterised as VUCA, which is further compounded by the pace of exponential change.[5] There are numerous macro challenges facing leaders today, including cyber risk, the Fourth and Fifth Industrial Revolutions, a volatile geopolitical landscape, economic challenges, the consequences of past generations not doing enough to combat climate change, the proliferation of fake news and a 24-hour media cycle. Each decade, new leadership literature is released, where authors (and I am no exception) pinpoint their time of reference as "now" being the most challenging. Has the world gotten progressively worse? So, why do people want to be leaders currently? Are they mesmerised by the LinkedIn profiles, obsessed with power and greed, or do they have a desire to create positive change and overcome key challenges?

Rittel and Webber, two highly regarded Design Theorists, coined the term "Wicked Decision making," which describes problems that can't easily be defined, have no obvious formula and are unique.[6] Wicked decision-making is unlike "tame" decision-making, which is straightforward and easy to achieve and closed off. Leaders are faced with making wicked decisions in a VUCA world, where data is lacking, they are time-poor, and a solution is needed the day before. There is no clear answer, and they often face poor solutions as the only outcome.

A Google search of top leaders will list out household names. However, for each one, there is a flaw, a blind spot or an experience of failure. Yet, each one of them decided to pick themselves up and still lead.

For every good or great manager, there will also be bad ones. Depending on their sphere of control and behaviour, they can leave an indelible mark. A recent, soon-to-be-published case study I have been working on focuses on PurpleCo. PurpleCo was a service company undergoing a period of change. A large and influential department had a leadership team that demonstrated poor management, which was described by many as toxic. The toxic behaviour in this case study led to poor financial decisions where vast sums were sunk with very little execution against strategy, as well as poor non-financial behaviour. Staff in the above case study spoke of suffering from anxiety and depression. Like other leaders, they faced the aforementioned macro challenges but failed to address them, such as harnessing new technology, which, as of the time of writing, remains an ongoing issue. They also failed to address key problems within their own business, to the severe detriment of strategic execution, financial performance and non-financial performance, such as their staff's wellbeing. When speaking to some of the leaders, they acknowledged some of their flaws, but they justified them as necessary. Victims from various fallout were seen as expendable. After a period of time, there was a leadership refresh.

I am not coming at this as a True Leader myself, although I aspire to be. I do not believe I was destined for leadership. Having had a difficult upbringing and being mediocre at school and in hobbies, I had no idea where I would end up. However, I liked to fix things, from a broken record player to an irrational operational process. Coupled with a natural curiosity and a gift for "persistence" until I had fixed a problem,

I ended up in leadership roles. Being comfortable in my mediocrity, I did not intend or want to stand out.

I'm not sure if it was the organisational culture I was in, defending myself against discrimination, coming from a challenging background, a lack of development at that point or just naivety, but I was unprepared and ill-equipped when I started out as a leader. I put in place some woefully inadequate mechanisms to help me succeed and protect myself mentally, physically, etc. This was definitely not a blueprint for success.

I always tried to be a better person and leader than I was the day before. So I worked hard to be the best leader I could, and investment in development has been key to this. I have both succeeded and failed. Some of my failures have led to my greatest successes, and some of my successes have sown the seeds for my most significant failures. As the Chinese proverb goes, "Success is not final, failure is not fatal; it is the courage to continue that counts." And, at times, it has been my "persistence" and courage which has spurred me on. I now refer to that time as a character-building experience.

Business analysts, when mapping out a process, start with what is called "the happy path." For example, the happy path of withdrawing money from an ATM involves the following steps: choose an ATM, approach it, enter your PIN, select the desired amount, and collect the cash. The unhappy path would be: unable to find an ATM, walk for twenty minutes, find an ATM, have a few tries before the card is accepted, forget PIN, last attempt was right one, not enough cash in the account to take out the full amount needed, choose a smaller amount, collect cash.

Many leadership books typically cover the happy path; this book, however, explores the unhappy path. Not that most of my career has been unhappy. I feel very blessed and fortunate to have not only done well but also had the benefit of such amazing opportunities. I have learnt from recognised industry thought leaders, travelled, walked the halls of the House of Commons, was instrumental in an industry-led initiative to support underrepresented talent, worked on one of the largest technology projects in the work, been involved in the launch of the first insurance blockchain, have collaborated on innovative initiatives with some of the most well known innovative brands or our era. I have been able to do a degree, an MBA and fulfil my passion for social change and charitable giving. However, achieving these LinkedIn moments took time and energy, and the pitfalls were numerous. This is the book I wish I had when I started my leadership journey. By helping you identify the pitfalls, or if you're in them, how to navigate out of them, you're gaining an unfair advantage over those who don't even know what to expect.

This book is designed to help emerging leaders consider leadership holistically, building on both the happy and unhappy paths, and ultimately achieve success. To learn not what it takes to be a leader, but a True Leader, because that is what we need now more than ever.

There are three shades of leaders. The main dynamic in this book is an exploration between two ends of the above spectrum, between a (false) godlike type leader versus a real human, flawed (with integrity) leader. And, what determines the anatomy of a True Leader, in reality the merging of both. This book is aimed at those who have aspired to enter leadership and are now at the inflexion point of emerging as a leader. This is the toughest part of the journey, marked by a series of new and exciting opportunities, as well as trials and tribulations. This lessens somewhat, but becomes different when entering the experienced part of the journey, when you're worn out, and then turning to think about post-leadership chapters.

By understanding the difference between what a False God does, as opposed to a Real Model, and being a True Leader who balances the two, you will not only be successful but also be the type of leader set up for long-term, sustainable leadership. We all know a few False Gods who have done extremely well, but their luck does run out because people don't like or respect them. That being said, there will also be the odd outlier, exceptions rather than the rule.

What This Book Covers

Chapter One explores the basics of why this book is relevant, why now and how an emerging leader can ultimately be successful if they follow the path of a Real Model or True Leader, rather than that of a False God.

Chapter Two begins by examining the key fundamentals of leadership, including the idea that people are born to lead, the importance of drive and motivation, as well as impactful development. I have coached, mentored, and observed numerous leadership development courses, and most are not fit for purpose. Emerging leaders have so little time; attending courses with no benefit will consume their already precious time. I conclude by examining external value systems and identifying what can help a leader thrive, or at least perform well, if the culture is not aligned with their personal values (which is quite common in large, corporate environments). All is not lost, but some skills are needed to navigate this in a healthy way.

In Chapter Three, I explore the next layer of leadership, including style, characteristics and other aspects. What are the main ones, and can they be used as a checkpoint to see if the right ones are being developed? Building on another type of development through coaching and mentoring, what the start of the leadership journey looks like, overlaying situational considerations, such as managing metaphorically in peacetime and wartime. There are several styles; it is rare for someone to excel at both ends of the spectrum. This presents an opportunity for an emerging leader to reassess their approach and ensure they are pursuing the most suitable opportunities.

Chapter Four is a deep dive into some of the behaviours exhibited by new leaders, as well as the tensions between happy and unhappy paths, including the pitfalls of high performance, ego, courage, confidence and doubt. I conclude by discussing the unrealistic and unfeasible rhetoric of being your authentic self at work, suggesting a professional yet authentic approach. This will help an emerging leader recognise they can learn from others who have gone before them, and not beat themselves up for being anything more than a Real Model.

Chapter Five drills down further into the types of challenges an emerging leader will face as they move out of the initial phase. This phase lasts until the transition to the experience leader part of the journey. Tackling issues such as office politics, machiavellianism, and what to do when you've lost the faith of your team, peers or management. These are the messier and unspoken areas of leadership; an emerging leader needs to consider where they stand, where they draw the line. They also need to consider wanting to be just "good" and not "bad", as purity of thought will leave them open to cunning foxes.

The golden thread of culture is woven throughout the book. Chapter Six provides clarity on key points and the crucial aspect of any leader's role: ensuring that those they lead are doing what they need to do to enable the organisation to deliver against its strategic aims. In day-to-day tactical operations, this is often lost, and before an emerging leader can blink, a year has passed, appraisals come around, and they are falling short.

In the final chapter, the book will draw everything together and lay out the anatomy of a True Leader, as well as the key elements needed for a leader to be successful. It aims to elegantly navigate challenges that enhance rather than hinder a career, all without losing one's soul.

Each chapter will conclude with key reflections and suggestions. Purchasing this book will also allow you free access to U-G-U's premium content, which contains a number of tools and guides to support an Emerging Leader on their development journey. The link to the online resource centre can be found at the back of this book.

Approach and Interviews

This book's skeleton outlines the leadership journey, drawing on academic research from renowned experts and current thinking. I draw upon my own experience of working for, with and within leadership teams across industries and geographies. From Fortune 500 firms down to sole traders. In addition to the collective wisdom of almost forty leaders who agreed to participate in a bespoke study. The group was mainly UK-based, although there was a small representation from the main working population continents. Two main types of interviews were conducted: a semi-structured question set of 14 questions and in-depth discussions of key areas. I sought diversity in various aspects to focus on the themes that support the above two dynamics and identify any main variations.

Diversity, Equity and Inclusion (DE&I)

Over 61% of the participant pool identified with at least one DE&I category, resulting in a rich and diverse range of perspectives. The three main challenges the group identified from a DE&I perspective were gender bias, ageism towards young professionals and bias against socio-economic background.

Industry Spread

Industry breadth of ten sectors or industries, which were: financial services, academia or education, health and fitness, defence, consulting, technology, hospitality, retail and media.

Some areas were not covered in the semi-structured interviews; however, expertise within the group included transportation, public sector and government services, energy and utilities, pharmaceuticals, manufacturing, luxury goods and law and telecommunications, all of which added further context.

Time Spent in a Leadership Position

The participant group interviewed had spent as little as months in leadership, ranging from a few months to more than thirty years.

The call for participation was for those aspiring to leadership, emerging leaders, and experienced leaders.

Aspiring Leader

An individual at the start of their career, typically engaged in education, training or entry-level roles, who demonstrates interest and potential for leadership. They are focused on developing foundational skills, understanding the professional landscape and are considering or preparing themselves for future leadership opportunities.

Emerging Leader

A professional who has completed formal education (does not have to be higher than GCSE) and gained initial work experience. They are progressing to roles within and up to middle management. Emerging leaders are refining their leadership capabilities, expanding their professional networks and assuming responsibilities that prepare them for higher-level strategic and managerial positions. Moving from this to experienced often involves an identity shift, which is explored further in Chapters Four and Five.

Experienced Leader

An individual in a senior-level role, such as Managing Director (MD), C-suite or equivalent, who has a significant track record of leadership. They are responsible for high-level decision-making, strategy development and influencing organisational direction. Experienced leaders are often regarded as experts in their field and mentors to emerging leaders.

No real trends stood out between the generations. Unsurprisingly, those with the most experience were the most comfortable in leadership and had the opportunity and time to shape the role to serve their needs, particularly in terms of time commitment, change management and industry citizenship. Those moving from aspiring to emerging cited the shift from doing and proving themselves to taking a step back and directing as a significant identity shift, and those moving from emerging to experienced called out the different skill set required, such as political acumen.

Correlation Between Age, Experience and Leadership Progression

The Leadership Participation group consisted of a diverse mix of ages and experiences. There was a clear correlation between age and experience.

The aspiring group consisted of students and managers, and it was the smallest of the groups. The age range for this group was between 19 to 55 years.

The emerging group consisted of senior managers, subject matter experts, leads and heads of various roles. The age range for this group was between 26 years to 56 years or older.

The experienced group was the biggest group interviewed, made up of the MD, C-Suite and NEDs. The age range for MDs was between 36 and 56 years, while for C-Suite or NED, it was 46 years and older.

The above roles are common career roles from student to NED. The role of a subject matter expert and senior manager can be confusing, as they can mean different things in different organisations. In this context, a senior manager is someone below a "lead," and a subject matter expert who may even be the same level as a NED is a person who holds that role, without the usual accoutrements which come with a leadership position.

C-Suite

Refers to the highest-ranking executive positions within an organisation, such as Chief Executive Officer (CEO), Chief Financial Officer (CFO), Chief Operating Officer (COO) and Chief Marketing Officer (CMO). These leaders are responsible for strategic decision-making and overall organisational direction.

Non-Executive Director (NED)

An independent board member who provides guidance and oversight without being involved in day-to-day operations. NEDs focus on governance, strategy and accountability. The Board will provide oversight and guidance to the C-Suite.

Managing Director (MD)

The highest-ranking executive responsible for the day-to-day operations and overall management of the organisation. The MD often reports to the board of directors and is accountable for achieving the organisation's strategic goals and financial performance. This role can be interchangeable with the CEO.

"Head of" Type Role

A senior leadership position responsible for overseeing a specific department or function within an organisation (e.g., Head of Marketing, Head of HR). These roles involve strategic planning, resource allocation and ensuring the success of their department's objectives.

"Lead" Type Role

A position that typically involves guiding a team or specific initiative within a department. For example, a Team Lead or Project Lead takes responsibility for coordinating efforts, ensuring tasks are completed efficiently, and serving as a liaison between team members and upper management.

Subject Matter Expert (SME)

A professional recognised for their in-depth knowledge and expertise in a specific area or domain. SMEs provide insights, guidance and solutions to complex problems related to their area of expertise, often supporting projects or initiatives across the organisation.

Manager

An individual responsible for overseeing a team or department, ensuring that goals are met, resources are managed effectively, and team members are supported in their roles. Managers typically focus on the tactical implementation of strategies and fostering team performance.

Student

An individual who is currently engaged in formal education or training, focused on acquiring knowledge and skills to prepare for future career opportunities. Students may also participate in internships, apprenticeships or part-time work to gain practical experience.

A study by Spencer Stuart found that the average age of a UK insurance CEO is 53 years.[7] Other research has highlighted that the average age of NEDs is 60.9 years[8], which broadly aligns with the leadership participation group.

Age, experience and role tend to correlate. Research suggests that a factor behind this may be the assumption that leaders in later age brackets have accumulated the requisite experience and wisdom to be successful leaders. This was echoed in the outputs above, specifically in the time spent in leadership positions.

The emergence of start-ups is changing the above dynamic, but not meaningfully at present. And one key outlier was whether the leaders could demonstrate entrepreneurship (beyond being innovative). One Participant had originally ended up in a CEO position in the age bracket below 25 years. Another consideration for this subset was that they often did not aspire to be leaders but ended up in leadership positions, driving their vision forward.

Summary

This chapter explores leadership not through an idealised or traditional lens, but as a complex, flawed and very human journey. It draws on insights from nearly forty diverse leaders, ranging from students to C-Suite executives, alongside academic research, pop culture and my own lived experience. We have all shared to help others – take this unfair advantage!

Leadership in today's world is increasingly challenging due to macro-level issues such as geopolitical volatility, climate change, rapid technological advancements, and operating in a VUCA environment. Leaders are often required to make "wicked decisions," which involve complex problems with no clear solution, limited data and tight deadlines.

Through deep interviews, I aimed to capture the shifts leaders undergo from aspiration to experienced, highlighting the mindset changes and identity shifts required at each stage. The research also notes that leadership is often shaped by organisational culture and follower behaviour, where even toxic leaders can rise if enabled by systems and susceptible teams. These themes, whilst nodded to in this chapter, are explored further in later chapters.

Reflections and Actions

- Some Participants shared that they had judged some of their leaders' wicked decision-making in a VUCA world, but this turned to empathy when they were having to make wicked decisions. What principles and tools will you implement to navigate this?

- Understand that leadership is not about titles or perfection. It's about preparation, influence and values. At an early stage, list out your values and boundaries.

- The journey will involve failure, learning and shifts in identity. The road ahead is long. If someone reading this is 20 now, based on current numbers, it will likely take 30 years to reach CEO – unless you have an entrepreneurial mindset.

- Beware of image over substance. What you see online (e.g., LinkedIn) is often the polished tip of a complex iceberg.

Chapter One

False Gods, Real Models:
The Anatomy of a True Leader

"The most terrifying thing is to accept
oneself completely."
– Carl Jung

The juxtaposition between a False God-like leader and a real, human leader lies in their core philosophies and the way they connect with others.

False God-like leaders present an illusion of perfection, projecting invincibility and omnipotence. They are often surrounded by an aura of superiority, manipulating perception to maintain their position on an ivory pedestal. These leaders thrive on dominance, image and the belief that they are beyond reproach. Their flaws are hidden or dismissed, and their governance is often self-serving, prioritising their power and control over collective well-being. To their followers, they seem untouchable, but this facade can crumble when their humanity inevitably surfaces in the form of failure or scandal.

Real human leaders, on the other hand, lead with humility and integrity. They embrace their flaws as a natural part of being human, using them as opportunities for growth and connection. These leaders are transparent, admitting their mistakes and vulnerabilities, which fosters trust and authenticity. Their strength lies in their willingness to stand for their values and execute their responsibilities with competence, even in the face of adversity. They connect with followers on a personal level, inspiring loyalty through their genuineness rather than intimidation or manipulation.

Historically, leadership has often been tied to notions of divine or godlike qualities. *The Art of War* is probably one of the oldest and most famous books, linked to leadership, and it "remains the most influential strategy text in East Asian warfare."[1] The work is attributed to the Chinese military strategist Sun Tzu, who has been described as a military general, strategist, philosopher and writer. For a book on War, it is not all about winning wars; the central theme is the character and activity carried out by the General, and that "character is the foundation of leadership."[2] The book has been adapted to fit a business strategy, applying its key principles to a business setting.

However, it was written when leaders were seen as having divine mandates. Attributes like "invincibility"[3] and "extraordinary" qualities[4] were hallmarks of leadership. Despite the evolving perception of the distinction between the sacred and secular, even modern texts from the last few hundred years describe leaders as "heroic"[5-6] or discuss "Messiah leadership."[7]

The term "False God" originates from religion and describes an entity falsely believed to be divine. Leaders viewed as omnipotent or omnipresent, and those who believe their own hype, become False Gods.

Characteristics of a False God

- Belief in their own hype and skill at creating it
- Perception of superiority, at least consciously
- Selfish, manipulative and corrupt behaviour that is often hidden, at least outside of their inner circle[8-10]
- No clear successor or competitor; they pull the ladder up behind them
- Bullying tendencies
- Questionable competence and capability
- Weaponisation of governance

If you recognise any of the above elements in yourself, it is likely that the more moderate version of it is being overplayed. For example, you have been told to promote yourself more, but you may have overused the promotion and now come across as being overly superior. Don't beat yourself up over it, but recognise when and how this shows up, and then try to moderate it going forward.

There is a further end to this part of the spectrum, narcissists, sociopaths, etc. This area is worthy of a book in its own right, and there are a few of them out there. As such, this book will not go further into individuals with these characteristics and dark psychology.

At the other end of the spectrum are leaders who possess opposite characteristics to those above, such as being humble, believing they are neither superior nor inferior to others, having integrity, being supportive and developing others.

Real Models, Not Role Models

The term "Real Model" has gained some popularity as a replacement for "Role Model." Unlike Role Models, Real Models are celebrated not for their godlike qualities, but for their flawed yet good leadership. They embrace their humanity, including faults and failures.

Real Model Characteristics

- Emotional intelligence (EI)
- Technically proficient
- Effective decision making
- Leads from the front or by example
- Respected
- Collaborative

Some people may naturally lean towards the above areas, but it is key to remember that they all require ongoing learning. The moment you think you have it all down and are knocking it out of the park, you might be leaning towards a False God belief. Nothing wrong with being confident, but be mindful of overplaying.

As Schedlitzki and Edwards, two leadership academics observed, "Leadership is often constructed as an idealised form of human endeavour, in a tone that suggests heroic beauty."[11] But leaders are just human beings. They are not gods, nor do they possess superhuman powers, such as omniscience or omnipresence. I must admit I am not keen on the current trend of almost anything being a person's "super power." It is great that people are celebrating their unique skills and abilities, but we are playing into this false, idealised version again. I have to ask: Is using this rhetoric setting us up for failure, either internally or externally?

Leader Follower Dynamics

The faults found in hero worship, however, do not lie solely with leaders but with their followers. As many academics have observed, "Leader-follower structure emerges quickly and spontaneously in most groups, even when a newly formed group sets out to be leaderless. It appears that whenever two or more individuals need to coordinate their activities, a leader-follower relationship develops naturally.[12-17]

The Padilla et al team, who are leading academics in leadership, along with Hogan (of recognisable Hogan Assessments), believe that destructive leadership arises not just from the leader but from conducive environments or cultures and susceptible followers.[18] Followers often perpetuate the False God narrative by demanding superhuman characteristics, which is why we need to stop playing into this. They often are the ones who place someone on a pedestal or tear them down.

Followship can extend to commentators, who contribute to leader narratives; some try to be impartial and factual, while others take a quite opposite approach. This has been shown to have a hugely detrimental effect, with news being weaponised, which arguably has been happening since the invention of the printing press. Judy Smith (of TV programme *Scandal* fame) writes in her book *Good Self, Bad Self,* "As a culture, we love to turn on powerful figures and are ever quick to demonise... people are always delighted to find someone new to tear down."[19] Participant 14 in the study echoed this sentiment, observing that in their industry, "Leaders get successful and then the market picks them apart." There is often little protection for either a False God or a Real Model, yet both groups display different tactics once torn down. The former styling it out, or at times playing the victim, until they can influence another set of victims or followers. The latter engage in reflection and learning, returning when ready, if they still want to lead. The problem with acting the victim is that it doesn't go very far before people become bored, which is unfortunate for actual victims who need compassion and support.

The fact that some Real Leaders fall at this hurdle seems a waste. Discussing this with leaders, I have received comments like, "Maybe they just couldn't cope; they weren't cut out for it." This appears to stem from a 1980s "survival of the fittest" mentality. Should this mentality still have its place in some industries today? Yes, but I think we have also moved on.

The 12 True Leadership characteristics that build upon those of the Real Model are as follows:

1. Strong emotional intelligence (EI)

2. Technical proficiency

3. Effective decision maker

4. Respected

5. Collaborative

6. Visionary

7. Inspirational in their work ethics and efforts

8. Innovative

9. Integrity

10. Leading from the front/taking a stand/being courageous

11. Wisdom

12. Cultural architect

Duality

Carl Jung believed that to become whole, we must face and integrate the shadow – the hidden, often less flattering aspects of ourselves. In leadership, the Real Model embodies authenticity, humility and integrity, while the False God represents ambition, presence and the hunger to be seen. A True Leader recognises that the shadow – the False God – lives within them and that the goal is not to banish it, but to harness it in balance. In practice, that might mean 90–95% Real Model and 5–10% False God. That small measure of shadow gives a leader the confidence to command a room, take decisive action and project authority when needed. But tip the balance the other way – 90% False God – and leadership becomes self-serving, performative and ultimately destructive. Jung's insight reminds us that wholeness in leadership isn't about purity; it's about consciously managing the proportion of light and shadow we bring to the role.

Summary

At its core, the book challenges the mythology around leadership. Using the metaphor of False Gods versus Real Models, it contrasts two ends of a leadership spectrum. False Gods are leaders who manipulate perception, believe in their own invincibility and often lead through fear or self-interest. In contrast, Real Models are grounded, self-aware individuals who lead with emotional intelligence and competency, embracing their human flaws rather than hiding them. The True Leader's archetype is built upon the Real Model's characteristics by adding wisdom and courage.

The narrative also critiques modern portrayals of leadership, sometimes by the leader themselves, and sometimes by a follower, especially through social media platforms, where success is often celebrated but the messy, behind-the-scenes work of leadership is frequently overlooked. Using Jeff Bezos' insight that success is often the result of years of preparation, the chapter makes clear that leadership is a long-term commitment marked more by challenge than celebration. This can take decades, unless the leader has developed leadership skills through entrepreneurship and often transitions into a leadership role.

The chapter stresses that leadership does not equate to morality. Bad people can still be effective (at least in the short term). This duality is vital to understand for those aspiring to lead or evaluating leadership in their organisations.

Reflections and Actions

- Recognise the responsibility of being a Real Model or True Leader. Success brings scrutiny. How you respond to failure matters as much as how you handle success. Model integrity and create space for others to rise. Consider the current VUCA landscape and examine various situations and scenarios, as well as how you might approach them.

- Where are you on the False God vs. Real Model spectrum? Are there any behaviours where your False God or Real Model part is out of balance? If it is, what might you do to check that?

- Culture starts at the top. If there are cultural issues, leadership style is often the root cause. Toxic leadership in one area can ripple across an organisation, as seen in the PurpleCo case study. What oversight do you have on the culture of your organisation?

- Do a self-audit. How are you preparing for the emotional labour, ambiguity and ethical complexity of the role? Mentors and coaches with lived experience can be particularly valuable in this context, as they can share insights into their own approaches that help stimulate your thinking.

Chapter Two

Nature vs Nurture

""Leaders are not born, they are made. And they are made just like anything else, through hard work. And that's the price we'll have to pay to achieve that goal, or any goal."
– Vince Lombardi

This chapter aims to look at fundamental emerging leadership dynamics. I have delivered courses, coached, and mentored for several years now, and in this chapter, I have attempted to address the main questions I am asked by emerging leaders at the beginning of their journey. These are questions such as: Are leaders born or made? What type of commitment is needed? I also include important development experiences. Finally, I address what is perhaps the most painful section for me, because I've been there. It's when hard-working Real Models come to me after performing exceptionally well, only to find their efforts unrecognised and their hopes for promotion dashed. That's assuming, of course, their manager has had the decency to be candid with them, rather than stringing them along for another year, piling on more responsibility without reward. I lay out value systems, and when there is a mismatch. I explain how an emerging leader can still thrive if they choose to do so. There is little distinction between the False God, Real Model or True Leader in this chapter, as they are fundamental to all; however, the False God will attempt to use shortcuts rather than putting in the hard work.

The debate between nurture and nature has been ongoing for some time. The debate centres on whether some people are born with certain characteristics or whether they are shaped by their environment. This chapter examines both sides of the debate regarding leadership. What I attempt to convey is that some people are born to lead, but that isn't what defines whether they become a leader or not. Several key fundamentals play a significant role, including motivation and development.

Leadership is a commitment, it's hard work, which is why drive and motivation are necessary. It takes time, but there are now many avenues open, not just the traditional route, which means needs can be met earlier. The portfolio career is starting to gain traction, and as emerging leaders explore alternative ways to lead, this could be an opportunity to find balance and meet needs throughout the journey, rather than waiting 20 or 30 years.

I mentioned in the first chapter the importance of development opportunities. However, I would say at least 50% of the information I got from courses was not helpful. It wasn't time well spent, and some courses were very expensive – two resources emerging leaders do not have. This isn't intended to be derogatory to anyone, and I have no bad intent here. But the onus must, unfortunately, fall on the emerging leader to understand the value and impact courses bring, and be discerning about what is needed and what is not.

The last fundamental element is something that comes up time and time again: the alignment of value systems and culture. Emerging leaders can still thrive with a mismatch, but a decision must be made as to whether they are in the right culture and how much they are willing to adapt. I mentioned not losing your soul, and this is one of the areas where it could happen if someone conforms too much over a prolonged period.

Hopefully, after reading this chapter on fundamentals and sharing the tools I work on with emerging leaders, they will recognise that there are plenty of fundamental tools at their disposal, which creates the right backdrop for them to succeed in leadership.

Are Some People Just Born With the Ability to Lead?

The debate over whether leadership is an innate characteristic or a skill developed through experience has long intrigued researchers. While environmental factors and personal effort undeniably play significant roles in leadership development, studies suggest that genetics also contributes.

The Arvey et al study, "Genetic Influence on Leadership Role Occupancy," was based on data from 646 male twins, examining the heritability of leadership roles. The findings revealed that approximately 30% of the variance in leadership role occupancy could be attributed to genetic factors, while 70% was influenced by environmental factors. This study demonstrates that while some individuals are genetically predisposed to take on leadership roles, environmental factors and personal development are more powerful.[1]

In the De Neve et al study, "Born to lead? A twin design and genetic association study of leadership role occupancy," it was found that individuals identified with the rs4950 genotype (approximately 25%), were associated with a predisposition for leadership. The study indicated that leadership, to some extent, can be inherited, but there are complementary mechanisms, like environment, but it is complex. This discovery provides a biological basis for leadership characteristics and supports the idea that leadership, to some extent, can be attributed to nature, although not entirely. The study concluded that future work in this area is needed, and it should involve examining both "nature and nurture."[2]

While genetic factors can influence an individual's likelihood of becoming a leader, most leadership characteristics are shaped by environmental factors, such as education and life experiences. Research in this area suggests that while some people may have a genetic predisposition to lead, the ability to become a successful leader still requires dedication, learning and practice. Leadership, therefore, is a blend of nature and nurture, with each aspect contributing to the ultimate development of leadership potential. As nothing more to expand on the nature side, the rest of the book will focus more on nurture.

Nurture and development are done "throughout the span of a lifetime" and will involve the role of "parents, teachers, work supervisors, etc."[3] Sadly, these roles have not always been nurturing. For example, Participant 30, whom we will refer to as Pete, came from a low socioeconomic background. He was discouraged from being a leader. He was told by his school's career advisor, "Nice dream, but that doesn't happen to people like me and you."

There is no clear list of "by doing X, you get Y." Obviously, good education, a caring family home and economic stability would be at the top of that list, if there were one. However, not having those things doesn't necessarily hold someone back, as seen in the case of Pete, who, apart from having a caring family, lacked many of those things. This is where motivation and drive can kick in, which they did for Pete.

Overall, the nurture side of the debate aligns with the feedback from the participants. Participant 2 shared that, "You can't train someone to be a leader, it is in you. [But], you can teach people techniques." These techniques include managing teams, creating a strategy, project management for delivering strategic projects, and professional skills such as building executive presence. When I work with emerging leaders who want to progress into leadership, we often conduct a skills gap analysis to identify their current strengths, what they are currently learning, and what they need to learn. We devise a plan to build those skills over time. To help consider different perspectives, we also conduct diagnostics to identify blind spots.

Four of the participants noticed leadership came naturally to them at an early age, whereas others were later motivated towards leadership. Except for the subset of entrepreneurs, the journey from student to Chief Executive Officer (CEO) typically spans 20 to 30 years, during which they gain experience and invest in their own development. The entrepreneur group was slightly different, with one participant entering into a CEO role in her early 20s. Also, most of them didn't set out to become a leader; it was while following their passion and during their entrepreneurial journey that they recognised they were leading others, and then worked on building their leadership identity by pursuing formal and informal development opportunities.

Personal Drive and Motivation

There are various drivers and motivations that lead a person to pursue a career in leadership. Some want to do good, while others, neither good nor bad, have ended up in a position of power. These individuals are purely status-oriented. Some may pursue leadership for more nefarious reasons. Whatever the reason, this drive needs to be as such; it will keep a leader going through both the good and the hard times. It is beneficial to consider early on whether the role will enable you to cope with the emotional labour it entails, not to mention its impact on your work-life balance. And, whatever you think it will be, add more in – this bit is always underestimated.

Exploring motivation was part of the interviews with the participant leaders. When discussed eight main themes became apparent (1) They wanted to be a consultant or coach, (2) aiming for C-Suite/ Non-Executive Directors (NEDs), (3) were not sure but exploring options, (4) were keen to go down the start-up route/ entrepreneurial endeavours, (5) focusing on financial needs for retirement, (6) general career progression, (7) stay where they were or (8) grow their business or the business they were leading.

Out of the participants, only one expressed a desire to remain in their current role. The rest indicated a preference for progress, exploring new opportunities or pursuing multiple options, suggesting that leaders tend to have a drive to be on the move. They look to progress, whether it be upward, sideways or onto another chapter in their life.

Over 32% envisioned transitioning into consultancy roles, often incorporating some form of coaching others. Studies indicate a growing interest in consultancy and coaching among experienced professionals, driven by the flexibility, autonomy and opportunity to leverage their accumulated expertise. A *Financial Times* article, titled "More Executive MBA students look to switch careers," shared that MBA students were increasingly using their degrees to change careers, with many moving into consultancy and coaching roles earlier on. "In a shift from historical norms, more MBA candidates are using the degree to reinvent their careers, not just climb the corporate ladder."[4] Participant 29 discussed C-Suite/NED options but cited a popular subject matter expert in their business, and instead preferred to follow this person's career, who was a subject matter expert and industry thought leader, in an internal consultant-type role.

Among the eight career themes identified, Emerging Leaders included either continuing along their current career trajectory or transitioning into consultancy or coaching roles. This type of group is often targeted for leadership development; however, only 44.4% expressed interest in progressing toward C-Suite or NED positions. This suggests that top talent has other options available and that traditional leadership pathways are no longer the sole aspiration of high-potential individuals. Consequently, talent retention is less secure than it has been historically. Talent retention research suggests that retaining top performers is a key issue, and organisations are now considering other approaches, such as enhancing their employee value propositions by offering more flexibility.[5] This should mean there are options, as organisations want to go the extra mile to attract emerging leaders. Supply and demand drive the job market, and this consideration should be taken into account at all times. Hopefully, the above serves as a reminder to emerging leaders that there will always be a demand for their skills. What we are seeing at present (2024-2025) is saturation in consultancy and coaching, which is being compounded by ongoing layoffs following COVID-19-induced overhiring, and organisations halting this type of work due to economic headwinds.

This study suggests that there is a diminishing interest in traditional career progression at the mid-career point; however, this group is at a juncture where they are more open to exploring various career avenues. Overall, the theme of freedom and desire for autonomy is a key motivator. I was lucky enough to have an organisational role which encompassed a wide variety of things I enjoyed. When I made the decision to leave the organisation, I underwent a significant identity shift, as I wasn't just saying goodbye to friends, colleagues and a company, but to more than just a job. Because I had a few things I wanted to do, I didn't want to put all my eggs in the same organisational basket again. I also wanted more freedom and flexibility, so a portfolio career made sense for me. I get to enjoy writing, coaching, mentoring, teaching, studying, consultancy and charity work. That being said, I am open to adjusting the balance or exploring alternative options in the future if my circumstances change. I am finding more people are starting to take this portfolio approach to use work to meet multiple needs and explore opportunities earlier on in their career, decide what they like or don't like, rather than waiting for a big bang, which they find out 20 or 30 years later that the ideal role was not what they expected.

The Experienced Leader group identified seven out of eight themes as potential career paths. Participants at the Managing Director (MD) level expressed interest in advancing into C-Suite or NED roles. Most participants in this group had clear plans for their next steps, with consultancy being the most popular choice, followed by exploring broader opportunities. This creates an interesting dynamic with competition between the emerging and experienced groups. Emerging leaders wanting to move to consultancy, but are not sure how to do so, crop up fairly often, especially in terms of how they compete with experienced consultants. What I have seen work well is the pairing of both experienced and emerging.

There were a few anomalies. Not all participants wanted to progress upwards in the traditional sense; one Participant wanted to stay deeply immersed in subject matter expertise. Participant 23 highlighted that they would prefer to stay in their current role. However, subject matter expertise, although valued, isn't financially rewarded in their organisation, and he entered leadership to reap better pay. He highlighted in his field that his experience is so rare, but the remuneration model only rewards upward movement in roles. Who is winning here? Neither the organisation of the subject matter expert. The organisation is forcing a knowledge gap, and losing someone highly skilled, having to then employ a less experienced candidate and wait for their subject matter expertise to develop. There are many good reasons for pay benchmarking; however, in these situations, this approach is not particularly helpful. Where there is a key reliance, surely it is more cost-effective and better for an organisation to have a mechanism to reward those who stay in their role, where they are adding the most value. In formal, structured organisations, this is hard to do, whereas in informal organisational structures, there is room to be more pragmatic. In either one, it is at least worth a conversation, as the old adage goes: If you don't ask, you don't get.

As mentioned previously, the Entrepreneur subgroup appeared to enter leadership as a byproduct of following their passion. This group did not appear to have a wind-down plan, but rather saw themselves as constantly exploring, enjoyed the breadth of their role(s), and remained excited about doing what they loved. Tamara Gillan was in e-marketing at Orange when she decided to strike out and initiate several entrepreneurial initiatives. She said, "The best way to land a dream job is to create it yourself," which might explain why entrepreneurs maintain enthusiasm and excitement throughout their career journey, because that is what they do.

Organisations are eager to retain top talent, particularly entrepreneurial and innovative individuals who drive growth, create distinctive products or offer deep subject matter expertise unmatched by competitors. They also seek multipotentialites – a term growing in popularity and explored by people like Emilie Wapnick in their inspirational TEDX talk "Why some of us don't have one true calling"[6] – adaptable, multi-skilled and creative employees who excel across roles, contribute both breadth and depth at pace and foster collaboration by cross-pollinating ideas. Despite this, most organisations are not designed to attract or retain such individuals. The above dynamic offers a challenge to organisations. Organisations need to rethink approaches to talent attraction and retention, and adapt to a workforce that increasingly values options, flexibility, and personal agency over long-term attachment to a single organisation or traditional career ladder. In my experience, organisations will try to retain top talent, and if an emerging leader can offer value in multiple areas, this can be a big motivator.

The Disneyfication of Leadership Development

I am passionate about the impact learning and development can have on a person. Whilst I have a deep appreciation for those in this field, there are limitations that have meant some courses, despite good intent, are not fit for purpose.

I'll situate my argument using a holistic development model. There are various development models available; however, the 70/20/10 development model is a widely recognised framework that integrates multiple elements from these models. It was created by Morgan McCall, Michael M. Lombardo and Robert A. Eichinger in 1996, based on a survey in which 200 executives shared how they thought they learnt. It is a learning and development model that suggests a proportional breakdown of how people learn effectively. 10% is more formal and structured learning, and involves workshops, webinars, e-learning 20% is guided learning through coaching and mentoring, and in addition, this can be supplemented with actionable feedback, joining communities of practice or other learning networks 70% is learning through experience, which involves secondments, "stretch projects", shadowing, and top-up learning.

As a person develops, they tend to start with classroom-based learning, then build knowledge through mentoring and coaching, and then learning on the job.

The 10% activity is generally more characteristic of the aspiring phase and less characteristic of the experienced phase. There is still learning at the experienced stage, but it is often more focused and nuanced, whereas earlier learning tends to be broader.

The emerging leadership groups are often where the 20% of activity can be of most benefit, and once the emerging leader has established confidence in their ability, they will often be invited to participate in the 70% of activity. In reality, they often span all three.

The entry point for early identification of being top talent is often through HR led talent mapping; however, this is not without the whims of bias, which can bar, even by accident, a potential leader. Essentially, an emerging leader will be at the mercy of a manager or leader, and that is if they have even had the exposure to be recognised in the first place. The key to overcoming this is to aim for early-stage stretch projects, often through self-nomination. This is where you are helping out another area of an organisation, which highlights commitment and hard work. It brings to the attention of leadership what you are doing versus what I call "jazz hands look at me," which is often a networking ploy and can fail quickly if the person lacks substance in their performance (most of the time, "jazz hands" is a trick of the False Leader).

Stretch projects and opportunities are a staple in leadership development. Leadership "characteristics emerge before the title, not the other way around,"[7] and it is often common practice that organisations will ask emerging leaders, who exhibit emerging leader characteristics, to lead without the authority and power that comes with a formal title. This is often a test of how they handle power and the influence they can wield without it. There is a learning curve to this, as the newly empowered emerging leader often needs to find their footing in the new role, which is not always done elegantly.

Organisations often have a taxonomy for job-type roles, typically ranging from entry-level to senior roles, including subject matter experts, managers, leaders and so on. These are in place to support talent and workforce management, as well as remuneration bandings. Below is a blend of typical role types. Organisations will vary, but essentially, the main types of roles are the Aspiring stage and the Emerging stage.

The Aspiring stage will cover early top talent roles, such as apprentices, interns, and graduates who are considered future emerging leaders, as well as supervisor-type roles and often first management-type roles. Early work placed assessments will involve talent mapping,

The Emerging stage typically begins when a person transitions from a management-type role or a senior-level manager who is moving from an aspiring to an emerging role. They are starting to do "Head of" and "Lead" roles. It is at this stage that an emerging leader may want to explore how they can get onto succession plans, monitor when development opportunities are available to build out skill sets, and seek introductions to future Executive Sponsors and champions, whilst building a network with their peer group (no jazz hands). The transition type role is Managing Director (MD) in a large business, or, if a small business, an MD is usually equivalent to a CEO, which falls within the experienced leader group.

An experienced leader can be considered emerged if they are at the MD level, based on the above criteria, hold a C-Suite or equivalent position, or serve as a NED.

The timing of development is important. People learn best when they have the right set of development experiences at the right time. A key learning experience is formal, recognised and accredited education, making an MBA attractive to those entering leadership roles.

Below is a table that compares standard MBA modules, the main components of standard leadership training and leadership capabilities identified by the Participant Group.

Standard MBA Modules	Standard Leadership Programme Modules	Desirable Leadership Characteristics
Strategy	Strategy	Setting a vision
Finance	Finance	Good communication
HR & Culture	HR & Culture	Adaptability
Leadership & Team Building	Leadership & Team Building	Leadership & Team Building
Innovation	Innovation	Integrity
Sales & Marketing	Sales & Marketing	Effective decision making
Risk	Technology	Leading from the front/ by example
		Emotional Intelligence (EI)

At first sight, the above disparity might explain why traditional leadership development does not support the evolution of leaders. Most skills in the first two columns would fit under the capability of technical proficiency. Whereas the eight capabilities on the right-hand column do not. There are some tangential relationships, for example, between innovation and strategy, as well as vision setting, which can be explored through skills building, simulations and other methods.

A good programme should build both technical and professional capabilities, helping the emerging leader reflect on and learn how to navigate the transition. Ideally, the support of coaches and mentors, and if in-house, possibly executive sponsorship or at least exposure to senior leadership, or a chance to network. I believe what should be a cornerstone of these types of programmes is simulations rooted in realistic situations.

Holistically, a mix of the above will help create rounded leaders, but if organisations solely rely on an MBA, for example, which has a sole focus on classroom learning, they are only hitting a portion of a leader's development. This may not seem too bad, but considering a part-time MBA takes two years, with the student working and studying often six or seven days a week, and the sponsoring organisation is paying for a full-time employee who is doing a variation of part-time work, the cost is quite high. Especially factoring in that the average age to undertake an MBA is around thirty, and they are expected to retain their learnings for twenty-plus years until they join senior leadership. This is why timing is an issue; the learning will not be as effective as it could be, as it may be too abstract, and much of it will be forgotten. This is where the 70/20/10 development mix can reinforce learning through organisational doing, and ongoing interventions can add layer upon layer of practice.

In light of the discussion so far, maybe the research from the Corporate Executive Board (CEB) begins to make sense; they estimated that "50% to 70% of executives fail within eighteen months of taking on a role, regardless of whether they were an external hire or promoted from within.... A survey of 2,600 Fortune 1,000 executives conducted by Navalent found that 76% said that formal development processes were inadequate, and 55% rated coaching subpar, if it existed at all."[8]

Ettore also linked the above research to that of McKinsey's Keller and Meany who found that "three-quarters of executives consider themselves unprepared for a position because of inadequate onboarding processes", the reasons outlined were not having proper training, that change in role and skills to go with it not embedded, "difficulties adaption to politics, pressure and expectations", don't prioritise "listening, learning and fail at managing change", and "lack cultural awareness".

Disney, the much-loved brand famous for bringing fairy tales to life through simplified, generic and compelling storytelling, is a commercial and beloved success. However, just as a Disney princess or prince story does not prepare young children for the modern realities of relationships, neither does much current leadership training adequately prepare a leader for effective leadership. All training is not made equal, and there will be examples of where technical proficiencies, holistic development and experience are setting up future leaders to lead. However, there are also some that are limited or well-intentioned but too rudimentary. Training someone to complete a SWOT is not the same as designing a strategy, or realisations on getting a team to bond and work together will not be found at the top of a speedily constructed newspaper tower (a classic training in team dynamics exercise is getting a team to construct a newspaper tower. I have had to participate in three of these, the first of which was in primary school). Confidence will not be built and sustained after a ninety-minute seminar, let alone when tackling issues like wicked decision-making, the real elements of imposter syndrome, or building coalitions with problematic stakeholders to effect unwanted change.

Research estimates that the learning and performance industry is currently valued at approximately $80 million and is expected to double in size over the next 10 years. Additionally, the global MBA education market is valued at approximately $47 billion. A huge amount of industry is in place for this, not to mention the investment of companies whose staff have time off to participate and complete these courses. However, as outlined above, if the courses are not delivering what is needed to help develop an emerging leader, let alone a True Leader, then what is the point, value, or benefit?

The UK government has recently withdrawn funding for MBAs under the government levy. While there may be criticisms of some MBAs, the majority provide a great academic experience for those who undertake them. Those in the Participant group who had undertaken an MBA all acknowledged that it added value to their career, but some said their MBA was too academic and lacked practical grounding.

Some larger organisations run programmes for emerging leaders, but not all. With MBAs now off the table, leadership development, at least in the UK, is becoming something of a black hole.

Leadership development was a theme discussed with the participants. The majority shared how they were continuously learning, and that learning "in the trenches" was key (Participant 27). 35% of the group had no formal leadership training. 23% had undertaken an MBA, and most thought it had helped them, but as one acknowledged, it is more academically focused and "not like [leading] in real life" (Participant 3). 19% had benefited from internal leadership training, but some acknowledged they had to push for it. 23% had received some training and/or had to self-fund, which was discussed with Participant 11, who explained how she identified areas for improvement and self-funded them.

It is clear from the above that an MBA is not the only way to go, and only a small portion of the group had received some leadership training. Perhaps the black hole is not as black, especially since it accounts for only 10% of the development mix, and the current model does not factor in the realities of leading. Others had developed on the job, in the "trenches" (which accounts for 70% of the development mix).

As per the development model, there are other types of experiences outside the classroom, such as access to formal coaching. However, this experience was not prevalent among the participants. Coaching is often viewed as a positive support for leaders; however, I have seen firsthand how untrained coaches can be paired with employees, with the best intentions, but at times create more harm. In one case, a Coach ended up competing for a role with a person they were coaching and used private information which the emerging leader had shared to gain the upper hand. Other examples have been instances where professional coaches have been brought in, but while trained in coaching, they lack the lived business experience to help with specific scenarios.

Where this is invested in through organisations or personally, thought must be given to what the Coachee specifically requires, the Coach's qualifications, specialism and lived experience. When coaching is conducted in an internal setting, consideration must be given to confidential matters and potential conflicts that may arise. This issue may be why the Navalent study found 55% rated coaching subpar, if it existed at all."[9]

A number of the participant group mentioned the role mentoring had in their progression, and all spoke highly of the Mentors they had benefited from. In most industries, mentors are typically self-nominated, more senior and experienced individuals within the same company or industry. The relationship can exist briefly to longer term, sometimes for years. The main difference between a Mentor and a Coach is that a Coach is there to help a Coachee develop a particular skill or change in mindset, whereas a Mentor uses their background, expertise and network to help a Mentee with any career challenges they might face.

As with Coaches, it follows that there must be good and bad Mentors. Participant 15 highlighted a risk: "If we keep doing the same old thing, we are going to get the same old leaders." This poses a risk from a mentoring perspective, especially if a number of False Gods are involved in these schemes and mentor emerging leaders.

The majority of the participant group shared how they were continuously learning through multiple mediums. There is a link between being a "lifelong learner"[10], situational awareness, and adaptability – all key Real Model skills. Participant 27 noted that "leadership throws different things at you and if you're not open to learning, you will get stuck or [your tenure will be] very short term." This theme is in most leadership books. In the seminal Jim Collins book, *Good to Great*, a leader reflected on his success, saying, "I never stopped trying to become qualified for the job."[11]

There needs to be a move away from Disney-esque approaches to something which will empower "True Leaders." Organisations should consider what this looks like for them. For emerging leaders, consider the learning paths which will benefit and set you up for success. A scattergun approach to joining everything is often a waste of time. Be discerning and pick one or two key interventions that will add value to your career or CV. Also, look for adjacent opportunities to network with experienced leaders who can serve as your next mentor, coach, executive sponsor or champion at the top table.

The Participants were asked what they think organisations can do to develop "True Leaders." They identified 11 areas: (1) training; (2) empower new leaders and support them; (3) let them fail, in a safe way, and don't punish on the first mistake; (4) provide a proper tool set, resource, infrastructure; (5) stretch projects to experience leadership before going into a leadership role; (6) pick the right people, for the right reasons, and coach them; (7) companies to be clear and consistent about what they say they value, what they actually value, and what they are rewarding people for; (8) create a culture where there is opportunity; (9) leaders already in position which inspire; (10) job shadowing; and (11) access to Executive Coaches.

Compare the list to the skills table earlier in the segment; the only real synergy is assuming "leaders already in a position who inspire" is the same as "leading from the front."

Clearly, with such a high failure rate, learning and development require more investment, a rethink and a reliance on less Disneyfied development.

Emerging leaders, take the development mix and the above list and see what you can implement. It doesn't all need to be done at once. As Benjamin Franklin famously said, "By failing to prepare, you are preparing to fail." It is very rare for an emerging leader to succeed without having a plan; even a False God will have some type of plan. For those who wish to progress, construct a 10-year plan and then determine the necessary interventions at each stage. I have created a Career Dashboard, which is available at the online resource centre. You'll find the link at the back of this book. This dashboard will help an emerging leader construct a plan, identify diagnostics to carry out at each stage and consider elements that are rarely covered in development, such as image, profile, and exposure. Those whom I have mentored and coached have all benefited from using it, and I have seen the progress.

Thriving and Surviving in a Culture, When You Don't Fit the Mould

Why do people tend to enter into a culture when they don't necessarily fit the mould? It could be due to necessity, such as financial constraints, a desire to fit in or the belief that they will eventually change the culture. It may be consciously done or not. When consciously done then decisions can be made on how to best proceed; however, when unconsciously done, the feeling of not fitting in might start with an internal whisper of the mind, the point being made explicitly to others, recognising microaggressions are not in your head, or performance management by a thousand paper cuts.

Generally, not fitting the mould comes down to a mismatch in values. For example, the social systems of large corporate organisations have a power or authority dynamic. The values associated with this are control, hierarchy and traditional leadership. If you are a person who aligns with a creative or artistic social system, whose values are based on originality, expression and creation, then you will not always fit the other mould. Knowing this early on will help an emerging leader identify organisations where they will thrive, not just survive. This does require a good sense of self and clarity on values. If an emerging leader is exploring their personality, numerous reliable diagnostics are available, and I recommend a free one, 16 Personalities, which can be easily found online. Regarding the comprehensive social system list and the values creation tool, these can also be found in the online resources section.

I often encounter hard-working emerging leaders who come to me, having excelled in their role – let's say in a power/authority dynamic – but have overperformed in an organisation's altruistic endeavours or creative projects. What they are rarely told is that they are expected to be altruistic and get involved in creative endeavours, and need to overperform in their actual role. It is because in a power/authority social system, they value traditional output; some of these managers do not even care about altruistic or creative endeavours, unless it benefits their performance. They consider it the cherry on top.

I suspect this might be a generational disconnect, where those in power adhere to more traditional ways of working, and the newer generations are seeking more purposeful ways of working. It will be interesting to see if the current emerging leader groups evolve in this direction or revert to more traditional ways of working.

Regardless of how a person comes to the realisation that they do not fit the mould, there are really only three options: you can put up, walk away, or fight back. Walk away speaks for itself. Some people believe that loyalty, being tough, and other qualities mean that when the going gets tough, you stay the course. There is a difference between metaphorically being in the trenches and fighting the good fight, as opposed to bleeding out. If a person is experiencing the latter, just as a medic would be called to the battlefield to tend to the injured, so too must a person in the work arena retreat and live to fight another day. The question of when to walk away is a tough one. It would be reductive to say that if it affects your mentally, go before you burn out; however, in my experience, by the time you have recognised it, you are going through it. Questions to ask yourself before you actually bleed out:

- What am I gaining by staying, and is it worth it?
- Can anything be done to make the role more palatable for me?
- What other options are there, internally and externally?
- How much emotional labour is it taking me to perform my role?
- How much stress am I under during the day?
- How much am I thinking about work issues outside work?
- On Sunday night, am I filled with dread?

If fighting back is the preferred option, engaging with a career coach who can help with conflict strategies is probably a worthy investment and will give an emerging leader the best chance of success. This will most likely be your first strategic dust-up; there will be others.

In toxic cultures or dynamics, it is okay if a person doesn't fit the norm who wants to be able to fit in with a group of bullies. In the case study mentioned at the beginning, PurpleCo, people did leave because of this.

The rest of this chapter will focus on putting up with this in the context of a healthy situation.

Putting up comes down to five key factors: core versus flex, adaptability, a strong cultural quotient (CQ), self-awareness, conformity and resilience.

The notion of core versus flex was shared by Cheryl Richardson, a leadership coach. The principle is that a person's core needs are non-negotiable, whereas flex needs can be negotiated. If a culture cannot meet most of a person's core needs, and/or is barely survivable, the emotional labour taken to accommodate, including the flex, will eventually be too much. If it is survivable and a lot of core needs can be met, and not too much flex is needed, then there is a likelihood that a person can thrive even if they do not fit the mould.

The key to flexing is adaptability. To thrive in a culture where an individual does not conform to the dominant norms and expectations within an organisation, it is a challenge, which is why they cannot take on too much emotional labour, as it will affect their health. AnthrOrg's

Culture Assessment Model (ACAM)® investigates the emotional labour needed in this situation within a culture audit, and the more required, the tougher it will be.

Adaptation is often necessary to function within a culture that may be unfamiliar. This involves learning the cultural norms, language and behaviours to engage effectively, while maintaining one's core needs. Thriving requires balance, ensuring that conformity does not lead to the loss of one's identity. A friend of mine mentioned how proud she was of her young daughter, Debbie, as she was good about eating fruit and vegetables – a parental brag, if you will, up there with potty training and demonstrating early artistic or arithmetic ability. At nursery, the Carers moved Debbie away from her friends into a different group that didn't eat any fruit or vegetables; they hoped this might convince the new group to start trying. However, Debbie ultimately conformed to the group and stopped eating fruits and vegetables. Years later, Debbie still barely eats fruit and vegetables.

Conformity is often valued for maintaining harmony, efficiency and alignment with organisational goals. A study by Gelfand et al highlights that high-conformity cultures in organisations tend to reward adherence to rules and discourage deviation.[12] This can create a double-edged sword. While conformity may ensure job security, it can also stifle innovation and discourage diverse perspectives. In contrast, low-conformity corporate cultures may celebrate nonconformity as a driver of creativity.[13] Whether conformity is accepted or punished largely depends on the organisation's written and unwritten values.

The Cultural Quotient (CQ) was developed by P.C. Earley and S. Any in 2003; it refers to the ability to understand and interact effectively with people from diverse cultural backgrounds. By understanding cultural clues and sentiment, a person can leverage their self-awareness and adapt in a more focused and meaningful way. It involves looking beyond the written rules and learning the unwritten rules of a culture to help navigate more effectively. Details on CQ tests can be found in the online research centre.

There is a requirement for resilience and strategic effort. While the journey can be demanding, it is far from impossible. In fact, many individuals not only survive but excel in such circumstances, often transforming their uniqueness into strengths. The caution here is that these are the exceptions, not the rule. According to Wood et al's study on authenticity and well-being, authenticity is closely linked to overall well-being and life satisfaction.[14] By embracing their unique characteristics and perspectives, individuals can build the mindset and tools required to navigate cultural expectations.[15] It is well-documented that entrepreneurs and innovators often leverage their distinctiveness to create new paradigms within new organisations or within existing organisations.

Subcultures may enhance a person's resilience. There are often several groups within larger organisations, such as fitness, innovation, reading and employee resource groups, which bring together like-minded people to engage in areas they are passionate about. This small subculture may support a person who isn't a stereotypical fit in the wider group, and they may be able to leverage this to help thrive.

While the strategies outlined above can pave the way to thriving, the journey is not without obstacles. Feelings of isolation, discrimination and pressure to conform will involve emotional labour. Building mental resilience is critical to overcoming these challenges. Creating health boundaries (which could involve setting milestones or planning for exit), practising mindfulness, seeking mentorship and coaching and joining more personally congruent subcultures are just some ways to help build resilience in this situation.

Surviving and thriving in a culture where one does not fit the mould is a testament to adaptability and resilience, viewed through a healthy lens. But, before you go down this route, work is called work for a reason. Why make it harder than it needs to be?

Summary

This chapter challenges the long-standing question in leadership development: Are leaders born or made? Drawing on psychological studies, real-life interviews, and professional insights, it is clear that while genetics may offer a head start, leadership is primarily forged through experience, motivation and development.

Twin studies indicate that around 30% of leadership tendencies can be attributed to genetics, while 70% depends on environmental factors, education, opportunities and motivation. Leaders across various industries confirmed this balance, with some discovering leadership early on and others developing it over time.

Vince Lombardi is a famous leader and football coach. His team, the Packers, won five NFL Championships in seven years, including two Super Bowls. The trophy now awarded in the Super Bowl is named the Vince Lombardi Trophy. No research was conducted on Vince

Lombardi's genetic makeup; however, he was known for his discipline, excellence and hard work. Research suggests that leaders are born, but whether it is genetic or not, they make themselves through hard work – that is the mark of a True Leader.

Motivation to lead varies; some are driven by a sense of purpose, while others are driven by recognition or a desire for status. The nurture element of leaders was explored in the chapter through current career pathways and development. The chapter critiques traditional leadership development pathways, including MBAs and corporate training programs, arguing they are often misaligned with real-world needs, and likens some approaches to the "Disneyfication" of leadership development.

Despite the significant investment in leadership development and education, its Disney-esque promise of producing leaders does not appear to be yielding the desired results. Organisations and industries should consider investing in these areas to support holistic and impactful leadership development. It isn't just about having the right leaders at an organisational level; in some cases, industries may be hindering their own evolution, echoing Participant 15's sentiments. This was an area identified by the Insurance sector, and since 2020, great work has been done in insurance between the main Trade Associations, to think of development at an industry level, such as the London & International Insurance Brokers' Associations (LIIBA) and the London Market Group's (LMG) focus on attracting top diverse aspiring talent. If the centuries-old insurance sector can do it, there is hope for all industries! Emerging leaders, don't wait - use the tools in this chapter to help your own development now.

Due to the current approach to development, emerging leaders are often underdeveloped or expected to lead without formal authority. Meanwhile, learning in "the trenches" and stretching opportunities often yield the most growth, but access is not done strategically, and where some thought is put into it, it can be unequal and biased. Unless part of a strategic approach is to reduce bias, not overload the more obvious talented individuals, and give access to those who don't fit the mould, or those who are diamonds in the rough, or those who are more introverted. How much someone wants to adapt and conform is down to them. My only caution is to be flexible, don't change your core, as you could lose a bit of yourself in the process.

The chapter also delves into an exploration of what it means to survive – and thrive – within a culture that doesn't reflect a person's values or identity, within reason. Consider your own values and the values of the culture you wish to join. How big is the mismatch? Resilience, cultural intelligence (CQ), adaptability and self-awareness are essential for navigating environments where a person may not "fit the mould."

Reflections and Actions

• Monitor cultural health. Does your organisation support difference, or silence it? Surveys are at best a snapshot of sentiment at a particular point in time; they do not measure culture.

• When considering talent development, go beyond MBAs and courses. Focus on more holistic approaches, such as simulations, mentoring, coaching and peer networks.

• Leadership is a journey. Build skills through experience, not just credentials.

• Leadership found some of your peers. How will you find it (or let it find you)? In exciting areas, there can be considerable competition. What is your unique selling point (USP), and is that something compelling to the social system you want to enter?

• Does your company have Executive Sponsorship? If so, how can you get on that programme?

• Choose coaches wisely; mismatched or underqualified coaches will limit your options. How will you assess quality? If the energy isn't right, then move on with care. Both the coach and the coached need to be adding value. Quick point to note: if you are on your third coach and not happy with any of the guidance, which all seem similar, consider the messages you may not be letting yourself hear.

• Consider the 70/20/10 development mix. How is your 70% being met? Are you being considered for stretch assignments? If not, don't wait for an invitation; it may not be coming.

- Understand your core values versus your flex values before conforming to culture, and as you approach promotion opportunities. Whilst leadership sounds good, there are practicalities to consider, such as longer work hours, increased pressure and travel.

- Do your cultural due diligence when joining new teams or organisations. I am a coach and mentor, and have observed the fallout from a person being punished for not conforming. Check out reviews such as Glassdoor comments. Awards (though not all) can sometimes be an indication of a company's strategy and a good marketing team. If you know anyone who works in the organisation or knows some of the leaders, ask them about the real culture.

Once you have gathered enough information, conduct some analysis (this can also be done if you are not part of an existing team). You can visit the tools in the online resource centre (you'll find the link to this at the back of the book) and explore diagnostics, value identification and creation, as well as various social and value systems.

Another quick way to analyse fit is to draw a vertical line on a piece of paper, representing you on one side and the group you are joining on the other. List down in each column some core characteristics and values for you, and the team or organisation on the other side. If you are not aligned, then there is a chance you may have some friction or not feel part of the group. If you are, then you should experience the usual team workings. The bigger the difference, particularly if the company is unwelcoming, the more it could detrimentally affect you, your career and potentially your health.

Chapter Three

Leadership Characteristics

"Leadership is not about titles, positions, or flowcharts."
— John C. Maxwell

Part of the leadership journey involves understanding what a leader is and the type of leader one wants to be. As a leader develops from management into leadership, the mind turns to the characteristics they possess and those they wish to enhance, as well as the skills of a leader they aim to develop. Following role models (or rather, Real Models) can help a person identify the qualities an emerging leader likes or dislikes as they work on developing their leadership identity.

A search on Google Scholar yields over 6,450,000 results of studies and papers on leadership characteristics. Clearly, there are many perspectives, and no single blueprint or definitive list exists. As Participant 12 said, "Good leaders come in different shapes and sizes".

The Emerging Leadership Journey: Ready, Steady, Go

As we have learnt, genetics does not guarantee a leadership career; other elements, such as drive, motivation, discipline and environment, also need to be factored in. In addition to what has been covered, two additional elements need to be factored in: accessibility and time.

It will not come as a surprise to the reader to note that leadership roles have not always (and, sadly, there are still challenges) been accessible to all. Primarily, those who identify as or are classified as a minority. Work is being done in this area with excellent organisations in the UK, such as Urban Synergy and the King's Trust, among others. These groups, however, mainly aim to assist aspiring leaders early in their careers, rather than in mid to later stages. So, once they are in, what helps them reach emerging leadership, let alone experienced leadership, is when Senior Sponsorship is active and/or reverse mentoring schemes are in place. Both of these helped accessibility in a sustainable way.

Pete (Participant 30) is a Managing Director of a few companies. By the time he was in his late thirties, he recollected, "People have a lot more opportunities today … I said to myself one day I will run my own business, will make loads of money and be successful." He was told by his school's career advisor, "Nice dream, but that doesn't happen to people like me and you." His workplace mentor, a few years later, said the same thing, but acknowledged that Pete had "defied the odds" years later. His businesses continue to grow from strength to strength. A great deal can be said about Pete's character and motivation. Komives et al highlight the important role mentors, guides and coaches have in leadership development, and a lack thereof can demotivate them to the point they don't carry on.[1] Luckily, Pete ignored his guides and backed himself.

Not only has Pete achieved leadership despite coming from a low socio-economic background, but he has also done so at a relatively early age in his 30s. This is quite rare, as the average age of a CEO is 53.

The leadership journey consists of three stages. The Aspiring stage will cover entry-level roles, early supervisor-type roles and often first management-type roles. The Emerging stage will typically pick up a person who is transitioning from management roles, or perhaps a senior-level manager transitioning from aspiring to emerging. They are starting to do "Head of" and "Lead" roles. The transition type role is Managing Director (MD) in a large business; in a small business, an MD is usually equivalent to a Chief Executive Officer (CEO). The Emerging leader can be considered as emerged and experienced if they are at the MD level, based on the above criteria, hold a C-Suite or equivalent position, or serve as a Non-Executive Director (NED).

The above aspiring group will not start participating in emerging leadership programs until they are approximately 25 to 35 years old. Taking an aspiring 20-year-old now in 2025, they would not start emerging leadership training till they are 32 (which would be 2037), and then assuming they reach the C-Suite at 53 years old, an organisation will not benefit from the above till a further 21 years later, which in this case would be 2058.

Development programmes that encourage executive sponsorship and shadowing can help prepare emerging leaders to hone their skills and gain valuable experiences. Succession planning is also key to assessing an organisation's full talent, with future leaders filling gaps to support development, network and agility, with the additional benefit of signalling to emerging leaders that they are in the running.

An HR function usually initiates succession planning. It is done from the CEO downwards. A method I am familiar with is the bench's approach. You have a bench for who can do the job now, in 1 year if they have the right development, 2 to 3 years and then 3 to 5 years. This is, in essence, a pipeline, and should be the focus of development opportunities to be worked on over time, overseen from the top. Often, emerging leaders who need an experience outside their direct area can be moved into another area. This is the benefit of doing it from the top, as emerging leaders can benefit from opportunities throughout the entire business. Alternatively, if a pipeline is full in one area and an ambitious emerging leader lacks room to progress, they may be able to benefit from gaps in another area of the business, provided they possess sufficient cross-transferable skills. Both the organisation and the emerging leader win. However, in smaller organisations or where it hasn't been established, an emerging leader, at an opportune moment – usually during an appraisal – could ask if this might be done informally. They might ask the leader if they have considered them for a succession role, and will support the requisite development opportunity. If the answer is no, ask what it might take for them to consider it. If the answer is yes, start working on a plan, such as a secondment, developing executive presence or honing presentation skills, etc.

Leadership Style(s)

There are millions of papers, books, articles, podcasts and more on leadership. From a research perspective, themes of leadership style have been defined by the work carried out by Moulton and Blake.

In the 1960's they developed the Managerial Grid. It is considered one of the most popular models in this area. The model has two dimensions: concern for people (Y-axis) and concern for production or tasks (X-axis).[2]

The five management styles are (1) Country club manager who is thoughtful, relationship orientated, and likes to create a good atmosphere; (2) Impoverished manager who exerts minimal effort, just enough to avoid performance management; (3) Middle of the road manager delivering adequate performance, balancing output with morale; (4) Authority-Compliance manager, who is very focussed on rule and compliance and can forget the people side of management; (5) Team management, inspiring committed people, working towards a purpose, operating well in a good culture. The widely held ideal style is Team Management.

This model is not without criticism, such as being called overly simplistic or ignoring situational context, for example, where a leader might adapt to another style to be better suited to a particular moment in time.

Participant 22, whom we will refer to as Harry, shared how they had attended a leadership course and observed two main groups. Group one was bold and brave, expecting their people to charge after them.

The second group focused on listening more, collaboration and being collegiate. Regardless of their group, "both felt insecure as to how best they could lead, and anxious that they should be more like the other group." Harry was of the opinion that there are different styles of leadership, both groups were effective in their own style and you have to be yourself and play to your strengths … stop being haunted that "I" should be another [type] of leader." This was also observed and reflected in the summing up, and "most of the leaders decided that they would stick to their own style as a result."

In today's multi-generational working environment, each generation has its own values, which adds further complexity as different leadership styles emerge.

My advice to an emerging leader is to recognise that one style will not suit every situation. In this respect, work on your core and flex. What Harry saw is important, as the style needs to embody you, and also how nuanced it can be, allowing for variations on a known style rather than following a book verbatim. It is easier to find your style and experiment with it earlier in your leadership journey than later on.

Another theme that emerged in the interviews was the existence of two diametrically opposed styles of leadership, one suited for peacetime and the other for wartime, which are more situational and aligned with cultural shocks. Leading in peacetime and wartime (metaphorically).

Organisational peace and wartime situations include, but are not limited to:

No	Peace Time	War Time
1	No debilitating activity	Time of upheaval
2	Favourable market conditions	Challenging market conditions
3	No Mergers and Acquisitions (M&As)	(M&As)
4	Stable leadership team	Power vacuums or unfit leadership
5	Good culture	Bad or toxic culture
6	No legal or regulatory concerns	Legal and regulatory investigations, breaches, etc.

Some leaders thrive and add value across a wide spectrum. I have observed that those who prefer wartime environments tend not to stay long in peacetime businesses, as they find the quiet environment too dull; they prefer excitement and the challenge of fixing things. Conversely, the character and skills needed for a stable peacetime environment do not translate well to wartime situations.

Recognising the time commitment of the role was discussed. For example, being brought in to turn around a challenging business may take 3 to 5 years. This will be a 5-year commitment, with potential for a longer term. Therefore, after 5 years, what is next? Exit planning is also important as a leader needs to know what they're walking into and how long it will take to execute their strategy. It may be that when the other end of the spectrum arises, it might be time to seek the next chapter of a leader's career. If it is very challenging, what is the plan if the strategy starts to fail?

Peace and wartime times are discussed in *The Art of War*. The link between situational awareness is woven throughout, but even the most experienced leader may fall foul of the current political landscape and the type of leadership favoured at the time.[3] Also, that great discipline is key. I often advocate the importance of situation awareness; the earlier an emerging leader can start developing this, the better.

Another theme is not fighting unless absolutely necessary, and only after less aggressive means have been exhausted. Sun Tzu suggests that one should only engage if one thinks they are going to win; otherwise, retreat until the circumstances are more favourable. War, mixed with even strong desire and intense effort, cannot overcome fatal flaws, and where there are flaws such as lack of resources or others… "a slow death is death nonetheless". This theme is explored later in chapters, as part of leadership is knowing when not to engage in a battle. Battle, in this case, involves taking on tough or risky new roles and projects, leader take-downs and strategies to force an exit on a peer, among other things. I have known many leaders who have mishandled this type of situation, and I have also been caught off guard. I sought the advice of a well-known coach who specialises in this type of coaching. A tough pill to swallow was recognising that I had inadvertently hindered myself in the situation, which weakened my position. I had also not developed situational awareness, and had I done so, I wonder if that outcome would have been the same?

A theme emerged from exploring this, not so much that wartime occurs, but rather who creates a war-like situation. Davis and Gardner explored the link between crisis and charisma, revealing a negative correlation between charismatic leadership and the emergence of crises – a finding supported by many others.[4] This mirrors the traits of the

False God, whose impact often extends beyond their own downfall, causing lasting disruption to others long after they have left. Often, the False God will not just be a problem to themselves, but to others, and their actions could ripple for a long time after they are gone.

Universal Characteristics and Skills

I have lost count of the articles I've seen on the "Top 10 Things Successful Leaders Do." I should imagine these are aimed at emerging leaders. Once they have established that they don't have to be born to be a leader, what must they demonstrate to be an emerging leader? As there are numerous sources on this subject, I carried out a meta-analysis, using AI, to highlight five universal key characteristics and skills.

1. Emotional Intelligence (EI)

2. Good Communicator

3. Adaptability

4. Visionary

5. Integrity

The above points help contextualise the exploration on the subject carried out with the Leadership Participant group. Two views were examined: What characteristics and skills did they think they needed at the start of their leadership journey, and did those needs change once they were in leadership?

Participant feedback on key characteristics and skills considered when they first started their career was (1) EI (all variations totalled 40%), (2) technically proficient and with expertise, (3-4) effective decision making and leading from the front or by example, and (5) respected.

It is no surprise that EI featured highly, as it often does in leadership research. Daniel Goleman popularised EI in his book on the subject, published in 1995. Goleman believes that EI is the key to whether leaders succeed or fail in their jobs. Participant 37, among many in the participant group, believes it is "essential." Goleman found that when he compared "star performers with average ones in senior leadership positions, nearly 90% of the difference in their profiles was attributable to emotional intelligence factors rather than cognitive abilities."[5] This suggests that 10% achieved success without it, or not as high as others, with some being incredibly successful from the start. Sometimes they have a False God veneer of EI, which is superficial or being used in a negative way. Luis Velasquez found that "people with high EI may be able to recognise and exploit vulnerabilities and insecurities in others. While the majority might employ this understanding for supportive purposes, manipulative individuals could weaponise it, triggering feelings of guilt, fear or obligation."[6] A False God trait. Anyone keen on seeing where their EI, or emotional quotient (EQ), is can access this via the online resource centre. You'll find the link at the back of this book.

Technical proficiency was cited as being important, which is not often emphasised in leadership papers, perhaps because it is a given. This involves either knowing the business or organisation, or the services and products being sold, or providing support to the business with subject matter expertise. Even in the latter case an awareness of the business, products, and services should be in place. Pete believes it is "absolutely necessary to fully understand your product. Unless you fully understand your product, you cannot lead the way. For example, you can examine the data, but you may get it wrong because you don't fully understand it. It is a pointless number." This echoes the strategic ethos of renowned Human Rights Barrister Amal Clooney: "You can't do the strategy if you don't have the details."[7]

Effective decision-making was also rated highly, which is not mutually exclusive from the above. In this context, it was meant to essentially describe what a leader does to help direct an organisation towards success. "Executives spend around 40% of their time making decisions, based on research from McKinsey."[8] With the dynamics of wicked decision-making, making decisions can be challenging. A series of incorrect, ill-informed decisions can impact the success of an organisation, or worse, lead to negative outcomes such as liquidation. Employees knowing they are in the capable hands of an effective decision-maker inspire confidence, credibility, and trust, not to mention other key stakeholders, such as Boards, analysts and investors. Sushi (Participant 14) shared some details about a Retail CEO, whom we will call Gordon, they had worked with previously. The company is a household name, once cited as a disruptor in the market they helped find. Sushi noted that the Retail organisation had been criticised in recent years in the press for poor performance. She remarked, "[the now ex-CEO] was not prepared to make tough decisions, and was perceived as not being prepared whilst trying to compete with ruthless [Competitor A]...in times of war, you need a general." Leading from the front or by example can be linked to effective decision-making, but there is a more fundamental anthropological and evolutionary factor at play here. Tribal leaders who demonstrated their ability to protect and provide for their tribe often by leading and showing high competency in tasks (which speaks to the technical proficiency point above), were fair, and had the capacity to protect the group, thereby enabling group survival, naturally stood out as leaders. This selection process was crucial, as "groups without effective leaders died out," and this survival instinct is still present in our "grey matter."[9]

The leader who leads from the front has a better strategy, can influence coordination with others, and ensures that followers are provided for. The followers, if there is trust and respect, will settle into their role.[10] A leader is metaphorically born.

Lastly, the respected point speaks for itself. Some acknowledge that people can respect the role rather than the person, and if the leader has the power to fire or punish, then they can still lead; however, this is a tenable yet fragile approach.

The second question I asked was: What are the top three characteristics needed, from an experienced leader's perspective? The genesis for exploring the two different perspectives stemmed from my own observations, which revealed that when managing emerging leadership development skills, emerging leaders often have a list of things they think are needed versus what they actually need, and these tend to vary. Often, technical skills gave way to people skills. Participant 18 explained the point well; they reflected that they wanted to remain as hands-on as possible early on in their career, but when they were promoted to the next level, they would always get stuck in, but it wasn't possible for them to remain as hands-on. "I am responsible for the people doing the job, instead of [me] doing the job...at a certain level, people don't expect you to 'do', my team would feel untrusted and motivated, and were being micromanaged." This is quite a common and early misconception.

It is clear from the analysis above that there is little change when comparing both perspectives.

No	Leader (pre-role) top characteristics	No	Leader (in situ) top characteristics
1	Emotional intelligence	1	Emotional intelligence
2	Technical proficiency	2	Good communication
3	Effective decision maker	3	Effective decision maker
4	Leading from the front/ by example	4	Leading from the front/ by example
5	Respected	5	Collaborative

EI (1), effective decision-making (3), and leading from the front or by example remained the same (3/4). Technically proficient (2) fell out of the list altogether. The new second-highest from the perspective of an in-situ leader became a good communicator. Respect (4) also fell out of the top 5, but did still feature further down, and was supplanted by the ability to be collaborative. Perhaps the participants felt being respected was a given at this stage, or that once in a position of power, people may not like the leader, but they respected the role, or at least the power which came with it.

When comparing the participant group feedback to the meta-analysis list of universal traits:

No	Leader (pre-role) top characteristics	No	Leader (in situ) top characteristics	No	Meta-analysis top leadership characteristics
1	Emotional intelligence	1	Emotional intelligence	1	Emotional intelligence
2	Technical proficiency	2	Good communication	2	Good communicator
3	Effective decision maker	3	Effective decision maker	3	Adaptable
4	Leading from the front/ by example	4	Leading from the front/ by example	4	Visionary
5	Respected	5	Collaborative	5	Integrity

There were some clear correlations between all three, and where different, some tangential correlations could be derived. Emotional intelligence emerged as the top performer across all three groups. Good communication exists between in-situ leaders and the meta list. Effective decision making was not featured, but tangentially, adaptability was (the latter of which is explored more in Chapter 2), which in part can support effective decision making. Visionary also appeared in the study but did not rank in the top 5. This is discussed more in the difference between Real Models and True Leaders in chapter 7. Integrity is explored throughout the book and is a key principle for a Real Model and True Leader.

After a more thorough analysis of style and character, it is now more apparent that the current leadership development cannon is not giving emerging leaders the experiences needed to learn or develop in key professional characteristics.

Despite the diverse experiences and multiple generations within the Leadership Participant group, there are some universal characteristics and skills that any emerging leader must develop. Growing subject matter expertise, developing people's characteristics and skills. For each character identified, there is no cheat sheet, or at least a credible one. Hard work is what will get you there. For example, take an EI test (available at the online resource centre; the link is located at the back of this book) and see how you score; where are you underweight? If your communication style is not working, consider why and with which group. In particular, Merrill and Reid's Social Styles might help you start unpacking this (as per above). Most good people have integrity, but what happens when wicked decisions come along?

The Power of Role Models and Followers

An element of the 70/20/10 leadership development mix is the power of role modelling (20%), whilst the role of the Real Model approach is described above (for the purposes of this chapter only, the term role model is used in the more traditional sense and aligned with the definition in the 70/20/10 development mix). This concept is recognised as fairly new. The point of this exploration was to understand the impact that role models have on leaders and what leadership capabilities, styles, characteristics, and so on, leaders might aspire to emulate, which is a basic but key way of learning.

The question posed to the participant group, "What famous leaders stand out to you and why?" aimed to explore role models and their impact. However, due to the wording of the question, it opened up more than just role modelling, but also leaders who are making a good or bad impact.

Thirty-one of the leaders shared their thoughts on good leaders, but some took a different approach, focusing on bad leaders and the reasons they stood out.

The research was conducted from December 2023 to March 2024. 2024 was considered a record year for elections globally, with "more than two billion voters in 50 countries" heading to the polls.[11] Overall, there were geographical trends in who voted right and left wing.

Perhaps this was on the minds of participants during the discussion, as politicians and those associated with politics in some way accounted for 42% of the identified leaders.

The Leadership Participant group was predominantly UK-based, with some geographic diversity, and a small US input. Despite this geographic skew, Barack and Michelle Obama accounted for 20% of those mentioned as modelling "good" role model behaviour, who made a positive impact. While exalted, most acknowledged they are not without their critiques and flaws.

Leaders who make a negative impact, such as Donald Trump and Elon Musk, were also highlighted.

Finalising the book in April to May 2025, Donald Trump is back as US president, and Elon Musk is stepping away from politics, having been heavily involved in the last few months. They have both been heavily criticised for political decisions affecting human and employee rights, global trade, and macroeconomics. A synopsis of how this plays out will be left to the history books and will not be further covered in this book.

Generally, based on the data, it was acceptable to have negative personal characteristics as long as you could deliver professionally. Those who were unable to continue delivering, having had a negative impact on so many, quickly lost support among their followers.

In an article published by the *Financial Post* called "Competent jerks – high performers who are horrible to colleagues – have a shelf life at the office," found their competency saves them for a time, "but when many of these competent jerks reach a certain level, their poor relationships and reputation, initially being impossible to challenge or confront finally catch up with them…fundamentally, people want to work with people they not only respect, but like."[12] This echoes Van Vugt and Ahuja's work, which found that people dislike feeling dominated or coerced.[13]

The concept of being liked was explored with Participant 26. He shared that there is a leader in their organisation "[who] isn't liked, but liked by the people he makes money for. He isn't respected, but he doesn't care. He is not in it for the love." If he stopped making money due to a bad call, would the respect he had be enough to carry him until he starts to deliver?

In the book *Good Self, Bad Self,* Judith Smith discusses a situation involving a person named Bill. Bill threw staff under the bus, shamed team members, and mocked ideas. His bullying didn't stop with internal employees, but also extended to clients. "While Bill was at the top of the heap, he won his employees' deference, but only because he was the guy in power. What he didn't have was their respect." After an acquisition, "Bill was pushed out. Because he couldn't find anyone with anything nice to say about him, he had a hard time getting a reference."[14] To those who have been bullied, belittled, or treated unfairly, karma does eventually catch up. "Anyone who has felt miserable at the hands of a competent jerk in the office, fear not, they will probably get their comeuppance."[15]

Positive characteristics that emerged included a leader's ability to do good, lead from the front and not compromise their integrity. Additionally, some leaders had a narrative that factored in some kind of struggle/overcoming a challenge, and winning over people who wouldn't necessarily believe in them.

While figures like the Obamas were praised for their authenticity and resilience, others, such as Trump and Musk, were polarising – powerful yet not widely respected. Leadership isn't always virtuous, and fame isn't always a reflection of admirable qualities. Figures like Donald Trump and Elon Musk demonstrate that influence doesn't require moral leadership. Instead, it can be built on charisma, controversy or raw results. However, their examples also reveal a quiet truth: Followership is powerful – and conditional. In a politically charged time, perceptions of leadership often reflected evolutionary fears, which are not lost on those using them for their own ends. Recalling Velasquez's findings that "people [or at least their advisors] with high EI may be able to recognise and exploit vulnerabilities and insecurities in others."[16]

Performance can mask poor character, but only for a time. The data suggests that competent jerks may rise, but their behaviour eventually undermines their influence and employability. Respect, not just results, sustains leadership.

As an emerging leader, consider who you look up to and whose behaviour you wish to emulate. I had a role model years ago, whom I had gotten to know over several years and greatly admired. Let's call her Petra. On a project, she created some problems, and I was somewhat disappointed with her behaviour, especially since I thought we had a good relationship. I was discussing it with my then-mentor Amol. My mentor asked me, "How many junior people has she brought up with her?" He asked me to name one. This struck me because she always said how much she helped junior staff progress, but I couldn't name one. Good leaders should be bringing up the next generation of leaders as they progress. There are False Gods who have very nice, shiny personas, but underneath, they may just be incompetent jerks.

Summary

Leadership involves ups and downs; it is a situational journey, rooted not in titles or job descriptions, but in character, skills, self-awareness and an ability to grow through experience. This chapter explores the essential characteristics, skills, and behaviours of effective leaders, not by offering a one-size-fits-all checklist, but by drawing on a diverse range of perspectives and research to reveal the complexity of what leadership really demands, as well as examining universal characteristics.

While foundational characteristics such as EI and leading from the front are key, communication, adaptability, and integrity consistently emerge as critical. The chapter also highlights other undervalued yet vital qualities, such as technical expertise and effective decision-making, which are often overlooked in mainstream leadership texts. These latter qualities are crucial for gaining leadership credibility.

The chapter examines the importance of understanding leadership styles and the significance of self-awareness. Drawing from models such as Blake and Moulton, as well as real-life accounts, it becomes clear that effective leaders are not all cut from the same cloth. Some are wartime generals, others are collaborative facilitators. What matters most is not fitting a mould but leading with clarity about one's own strengths and weaknesses.

A powerful analogy that runs through the chapter is that of leading in "peacetime" versus "wartime." The chapter outlines how effective leadership requires contextualisation. Characteristics that serve well in calm, stable environments, such as collaboration and consensus, may falter in crisis, where decisiveness, strategic aggression, and resilience are paramount. The ability to sense the environment and adjust leadership style accordingly is essential to long-term success. Not every leader will have the dexterity to lead at both ends of the spectrum.

A key message here is that leaders must give themselves permission to lead in a way that aligns with their authentic selves. Style is personal, not prescriptive. This must be rooted in the culture they are working in and being workthentic.

As leaders transition from aspiration to emerging, the skills they need also evolve. Characteristics they once saw as essential, such as technical expertise and being respected, often shift in priority, replaced by more people-oriented skills, including collaboration and communication, as they begin to lead teams and manage broader agendas. Yet, foundational characteristics like EI, integrity, and adaptability remain constant, underlining the importance of early development cornerstones. The chapter proposes that future leaders should begin developing these characteristics well before they assume formal leadership roles. This can be supported by more holistic and immersive leadership development programmes.

Role models play a significant role in shaping one's leadership identity. Some are admired for overcoming adversity and leading with depth and conviction, while others, like competent jerks, are tolerated only temporarily. The chapter warns that performance alone is not enough; long-term leadership credibility requires respect, trust, and relational intelligence.

The chapter also confronts the issue of leadership accessibility. Through Pete's story, he shares his experience, illustrating how early bias and limited access to leadership development can delay or block the rise of capable leaders, especially those from underrepresented or disadvantaged backgrounds. It challenges current leadership pipelines, pointing out that if aspiring talent isn't identified and nurtured earlier, sectors can face a 20-year or longer gap before benefiting from diverse leadership. This is the time period of the emerging leader. Very little is done to support talent over the decades until they get to leadership, and there are many barriers to getting there, which are abundant in the current underrepresented minorities. Most argue against diversity hires, and putting the wrong person in the job is indeed wrong; however, opening up talent pools to underrepresented talent does need to be done. There is a greater risk to maintaining limited talent pools, where there may be no alternative but to hire the wrong person, as there is so little to choose from – essentially picking the best of the worst.

Ultimately, the chapter reinforces that leadership is not about a title or managing tasks; it's about earning trust, making decisions under pressure, and influencing people toward a shared purpose. The journey to leadership is open to all. It's when emerging leaders start to get tested that the False God will eventually be exposed, but for the Real Model or True Leader, it demands intentionality, growth, and adaptability. Whether in peace or crisis, True leadership is rooted in clarity of character, self-awareness and the courage to lead from who you are, not who you think you should be.

Reflections and Actions

- Own your leadership identity. Leadership is a journey rooted in self-awareness. Lead from who you are.

- Prioritise emotional and relational skills alongside technical expertise. Your ability to influence, adapt and inspire matters more as your scope of responsibility grows. Utilise tools and simulations to identify areas that require improvement. Honing skills earlier on, will make the emerging leadership journey smoother and more successful.

- Prepare for situational leadership. Understand that leading in stable times ("peacetime") and crisis ("wartime") demands different mindsets, which one do you survive and thrive in?

- Recognise leadership starts before the title. Leadership is often exercised in small moments of influence, rather than through formal authority.

- Choose to lead where you are. Whether in communities, workplaces or families, leadership is a choice and a responsibility available to everyone.

- Don't fall for the romanticised ideal of leadership on LinkedIn. When picking role models, mentors and coaches, don't pick the disguised False God; it could be your undoing later on in your career.

Chapter Four

I Think, Therefore I Lead

"To lead is first to know oneself;
to think deeply is to guide with purpose."
– Soren Kierkegaard, inspired by Aristotle

As we move away from nature versus nurture, development and the more fundamental characteristics of leadership, we often find there is an inner transformation to be undertaken. Maybe less for a False God who believes they are entitled to lead, but more for the Real Model who can then go on to develop into a True Leader, and have sustained success.

Descartes famously said, "I think, therefore I am." The core of the idea is that a person's ability to think is undeniable proof that they exist, at least in some form. As emerging leaders transition from management to leadership, moving beyond the fundamentals and basic considerations involves them clarifying what leadership means to them and how they can effectively lead. In this case, they utilise the Descartesian thinking of "I think I am a leader, therefore I am a leader" in at least some form. At some point, the manager realises they need to morph into a leader.

However, when real life and philosophy intersect, a mental battle ensues.

How does the thought become the father of the wish? Sometimes all that is needed is permission to lead. This can be done through the reward of a job title, which can be powerful, though not the be-all and end-all. A study by Susan Komives et al titled "A Leadership Identity Development Model: Applications from a Grounded Theory" found that labelling people as leaders made a difference. One of their participants was quoted as saying, "I feel more authorised to go ahead."[1]

In the excellent book, *Act Like a Leader, Think Like a Leader*, Herminia Ibarra, an expert on professional leadership and development, found that leaders become leaders by doing the work. She coined the term "outsight," which refers to a cycle of "acting like a leader and then thinking like a leader," as excessive thinking before taking action can be limiting. This sounds a bit counterintuitive, but what she is driving at is that most people wait until they feel like leaders before they start acting like one. By then, however, it might already be too late. Her point is that leadership identity doesn't just emerge from reflection or planning; it grows through action. She has a very future-focused approach around building out a new network to help expand horizons, "envisioning new possibilities," and not coming to leadership from limited and dated perspectives.[2]

This new chapter in a person's life often involves an identity shift, as often what has got the manager to this point (e.g. being a reliable workhorse) becomes less about doing and more about compelling, inspiring or getting others to do. This theme comes up in my own coaching business regularly, and the work being done can be quite deep.

It is not the time to take old wounds and outdated frameworks with you. A new leader needs to evolve and adapt to their new landscape.

As a person calibrates into a leadership role, then, as with any identity shift, the new landscape may not be right for them. Some choose to happily go back to management, which is why leadership simulations, as part of leadership development, can help emerging leaders understand the day-to-day of leadership and not the romanticised version. The day-to-day involves time spent on governance, meetings and cat herding. It can take many years to get into leadership mode. If tasters can be done earlier on it can benefit the person and the organisation.

The Emerging Leadership Journey: And We're Off

A new leadership identity typically develops in 12 to 18 months. Komives et al compiled a Leadership Identity Development Model (LID) based on their study of leadership in students. They define six stages, which are not necessarily linear and at times cyclical:[3]

1. Awareness

2. Exploration/Engagement

3. Leader identified

4. Leadership differentiated

5. Generativity

6. Integration/Synthesis

"Each stage ends with a transition that signals the beginning of the next stage. The transition marked a shift in thinking, a gradual process of letting go of old ways of thinking about leadership to trying new ways. Transitions mark more reflective than active periods. Students signalled the readiness to shift toward the next stage, without yet having complete access to the thoughts or behaviours of the next stage. The emerging phase encompassed an experimental adoption of the new ways of being and thinking. In this phase, the student was "trying on" the new way of being, often tentatively. The immersion phase signalled greater ease in the stage, a time to practice the new stage, and a more complete adoption of the new way of exercising leadership, including the use of new skills."[4]

Essentially, a leader doesn't develop overnight; it takes time, reflection, and meaningful experiences.

In the paper titled "Who Will Lead and Who Will Follow," Douglas Scott DeRue and Susan Joy Ashford state that an emerging leader may think and then "claim" a leadership role, but a process of mirroring and reinforcement must be met by followers who "grant" it. Failure to do so will not enable a leader-follower relationship to develop.[5] This can be very hard when being asked to lead without authority, or when leading a team that the emerging leader was once in. Both scenarios may contain resistance.

The next element after believing you are a leader and creating your leadership identity is building followership. This is one of the hardest areas to develop and is a shift I work on with a lot of coaches and mentees.

Whilst creating something new, some other things need to be let go of. The leader will often need to let go of the expert and start to be the enabler of their teams and/or followers. Despite the recognition they got from doing, they need to move from doing to guiding. This can be especially hard as it was often this that got the leader a promotion in the first place.

Imposter syndrome may begin to manifest as the new identity develops. I have laid out some key elements of a mental process, which could be of help, below:

1. Do you trust yourself? Self-trust = integrity + resilience + showing up for yourself consistently + self-awareness.

2. Are you able to trust others and build trust between each party? Those who are more cynical in nature or perfectionists should consider how far they want to take this approach. It isn't about sustaining additional emotional labour; there is no choice but to let go of the old. A coach specialising in identity shifts can be helpful in this area.

3. In the new world, a leader's span of control will widen, and you will not be able to control everything; therefore, you need to make peace with any desire you have to control any of it (this is why governance is so key). Often, it will be fear driving this, fear of failing, being judged, etc. An experienced leader's secret about fear of failing is that your fear will come true. You will fail, and people *will* judge you – it's part of the gig.

4. When a person is under pressure, they will naturally go back to controlling and doing tendencies, if this is a default behaviour.

The key is to recognise triggers and challenge inner narratives. If you have been travelling and are tired or jet-lagged, being bombarded with five different wicked decisions and stressed about a problem at home, it will force you to rely a lot on your resilience. Resilience is not infinite. Recognise you are over-taxed and perhaps have a break, leave a bit earlier (or at least on time), schedule time for wicked decision-making tomorrow where possible.

5. For a team to perform, they must feel psychologically safe. As a leader, it is up to you to create it. Any fear you are internalising must be addressed until you, as a leader, feel safe. Being a leader is now about enabling others, which may be hard to do if you're very new to leadership. How can a new emerging leader trust their new identity as it develops and feel safe when there isn't a current anchor? Trust in yourself and accept the process; you will get there.

6. Do the other team members know what they need to deliver to succeed? Some questions to ask them may be as follows:

   a. Are they in the right role?

   b. Do they have clarity on what is being delivered, and the how, the what and the why of it?

   c. Have you put in the appropriate boundaries and systems for management and oversight?

The above introduces a new way of thinking: Just go through the process each time, until you are automatically doing it, and it becomes a habit. Once the above cycle has been broken, it becomes a smoother process to start thinking in terms of not just the team winning, but together means the success of the organisation.

At each new start, confidence will need to be recalibrated. This is why characteristics such as adaptability and being comfortable with ambiguity are helpful. I am often presented with Coachees and Mentees who say they have no confidence. This internal dialogue is not helpful as they believe they are bereft of total confidence. In most cases, it's not a major issue – just a small problem that feels like a big block, usually caused by a hit to situational confidence during an identity shift. Once identified, it can be worked on and resolved. Core confidence problems are often deeper and tend to benefit from a different approach.

Core vs. Situational Confidence

Core confidence ((self-belief x past mastery x self-compassion)/fear of failure)) is believing you can handle a situation, within reason, and being healthy enough to know when it can't be handled. You are trusting in yourself that whatever happens, you can respond, adapt, learn and move on. If you've made it this far, you may just need a little help.

Situational confidence ((preparation x experience x support)/situational stress)) is context-specific and will be triggered if you're stepping into a new role, especially a 70% stretch role. This *will* happen, so expect to be triggered. At this point, lean back into your core confidence. Look at the elements of the equation: Can you meet these? If not, then put something into place. Define what success looks like – not utopian success but real and pragmatic success – and start meeting and acknowledging tiny wins to help build confidence as the new identity is anchoring.

There is no race to the finish line. The inner work of leadership can be deep for some. This is why we need to move beyond Disney-fied development into holistic development.

This segment, along with the rest of this chapter, examines key experiences of a person on an internal journey to becoming an emerging leader. Leadership identity is not fixed on day one, but rather is a dynamic, evolving process built through experience, reflection and relationships with others. The challenge isn't just in the day job, but also in other elements, such as impostor syndrome, fear of failure and control reflexes surfacing, especially in new roles where people recalibrate both their identity and confidence.

A Real Model will embrace vulnerability and rawness – not necessarily openly – but will explore it, do the work to let go of the past and old ways, and do their best for their team/organisation. They will nurture core confidence and employ resilience to become comfortable with situational confidence – not to fall into the unhealthy belief that all challenges can be met, but stretch themselves enough to take on new and appropriate challenges. This is when they start to become a True Leader.

The High-Performing Leader: A Story of Workaholism and Recovery from Perfectionism

Let us imagine Aamina, a woman in her early career. Aamina was recognised for having above-average competence and a good work ethic, as well as being a strategic thinker. She quickly rose through the ranks, being promoted into leadership positions far earlier than most of her peers. Her drive for excellence was unmatched, bordering on pedantry, and she consistently delivered extraordinary results.

Among the characteristics that defined her as a high performer were ambition, resilience, adaptability and uncompromising standards. But what most shaped her success – and her struggle – was perfectionism, the relentless pursuit of flawlessness, coupled with exceedingly high standards and a critical self-evaluation process. The underlying factor was a fear of losing control, including the loss of one's reputation and similar consequences. In a desperate attempt to avoid fear, she convinced herself into workaholism.

The benefits to the organisation were high standards, drive to succeed, and continuous improvement, but the problems were that she had unrealistic expectations of herself and others; during periods of high stress, she could strain relationships. But as she kept winning, she didn't see the need to change – and the organisation didn't want her to. The higher up she went, the bigger the work challenges, coupled with higher expectations. The breaking point came when Aamina's health began to suffer. The constant pressure to maintain her standards and stick to ambitious deadlines led her to the brink of burnout. She realised she was pushing herself even harder than she pushed her teams. But when things got tougher, she dug in deeper, tying herself to further improved productivity.

Aamina was then promoted to another leadership position. Her new manager, Paul (her first Real Model), recognised the route she was going down. He gently coached her to understand the impact she was having on herself and her teams. Through coaching, Aamina came to understand that her perfectionism, while a strength in many ways, was also her greatest weakness. Paul helped her find a professional coach who worked with her to uncover the root of her drive and its impact on herself and others.

She eventually adopted a recalibrated leadership style of kindness to herself, which then translated to teams, and consequently resulted in a more balanced approach to commitment and delivery. She discovered that success isn't defined by perfectly polished flawlessness, but by progress and adaptability. She couldn't entirely eliminate her default, but she could accept it, learn to recognise it, and moderate it. In her evolution, Aamina became not just a leader but an empathetic Real Model, proving that even the highest achievers can grow by embracing imperfection. It also changed her leadership style. She made room for her new leadership identity and started to develop further, unlocking the career plateau she had remained stuck at.

The above story is a blend of anecdotes and the lived experiences of other leaders. It is a little bagatelle to remind those who claim to be perfectionists, when asked about their worst characteristics, that this is actually one of them.

Burnout can manifest in various forms; it won't just be a result of extended hours. Sometimes, utilising emotional labour long-term can be just as damaging. Worst case, it can lead to prolonged and serious health conditions. Japan and South Korea have reported deaths officially attributed to overwork, often after 80–100+ hour working weeks.

Real models will work hard. This is a rare occasion when looking at a False Leader can help. Yes, I said it. You will never see a False God working long hours or staying in a situation which doesn't add any value to them. Consider this approach: Don't become a False God. Look at the logic they are applying and consider whether everything you are doing is really adding value to you and to others.

When working with emerging leaders, the advice I often give is this: A first leadership job will often be a stretch; how will you expect to perform well or progress when you have burnt yourself out getting there?

Leadership & Ego

Various connotations can be applied to the word ego. Colloquially, it often involves a negative connotation in everyday life, e.g. "X is so egotistical."

Like many concepts in this book, ego is also on a spectrum: from unhealthy (more often than not a False God) to healthy (most likely a Real Model or True Leader). This will be one of the areas where the designations on each end of the spectrum are not as clear-cut, and where some Real Models might need to accept, however small, that they have an element of a False God. "Confidence has an evil twin that derails success – arrogance."[6]

Some of the more status-driven leaders will see positive benefits from their role, such as adoration, public recognition and fantastic pay. People immediately think they are superior. It's hard to imagine that even the humblest leader wouldn't get their head turned, at least a little, in the beginning. These are all responses to power and a popularity bias – a bias where people assume that someone must be good, right and competent/valuable simply because of their title, or is popular, regardless of their full character or ability. When a leader becomes caught up in this bubble, their ego can become inflated, confidence overflows, humility is forgotten, and arrogance sets in. "Overconfidence…has been blamed for wars, stock market bubbles, strikes, unnecessary lawsuits, high rates of entrepreneurial bankruptcy, and the failure of corporate mergers and acquisitions."[7]

> "There is plenty of research to show that [an unhealthy] ego is a hugely damaging force in the workplace and team/leader cohesion … A 2009 survey of over 1,200 employees by Florida State University …. Found that 31% of participants reported that their superior exaggerated their accomplishments to look good. 27% said their boss bragged to get praise. 25% believed that the person in charge had an inflated view of themselves. 24% thought their boss was self-centred."[8]

In Jim Collins' book *Good to Great*, he lays out a 5-level model for leadership. Level 5 represents the idea: a leader who builds greatness and success through will, skill and humility. Ego – meant in the colloquial sense – or rather, the lack of it, is what Collins lists as one of the markers of a level 5 leader. Failing to manage or check this can lead to organisational cultural toxicity and chaos.[9]

Ego and arrogance were explored with the Participant Leadership group. They were asked if they had ever let their ego run amok or seen a fellow leader do so. All answered yes – often with a smile or a laugh. A few leaders acknowledged they could be arrogant from time to time, but didn't see themselves as arrogant people.

Arrogant behaviours cited include:

- Overconfidence
- Thinking they are better than others /acting superior
- Punishing others, especially if they fear someone is more knowledgeable than them
- Acting unfairly or aggressively
- Not admitting fault
- Micromanaging and creating bottlenecks in the business
- Being self-serving
- Acting independently and ignoring peer counsel ("I know better")
- Bullying
- Cowardly behaviour when a stand is needed but not politically expedient

Everyone has confidence and ego, but whether it consumes them – and leads them to become arrogant or self-serving – depends on the individual. This can create a problem with followership – the people an emerging leader needs to lead – because arrogance can be off-putting. Participant 18 said that they had "never met an arrogant person, who was good, liked and respected."

Sushi (Participant 14) shared some lived experience about a leader she worked with who, for the most part, aligned with a False God archetype. It is in these stories that the boundaries between the two are blurred. Leadership is not simplistic; it is nuanced, complex, and layered. Hank (the Chief Executive Officer or CEO) had almost a "mythic career… he was allegedly trained for this and that, won X and Y, etc. We worked out once that if he had achieved all of these things, he would be over 300 years old."

But Sushi also acknowledged that the things she saw Hank achieve were incredible: "He was like a shot of adrenaline [to the organisation] and we did start to make money." This was not the only layer to him. He also empowered and challenged others; he was "inspiring… he came in with the desire to make the world a better place." Outside of work, he exhibited kindness and altruism (no fauxlanthropy—it was done out of the public eye). But his success came to the detriment of psychological safety. Even during peacetime, people were "scared of him," including his top team.

Under Hank's layered leadership style, the organisation initially became more successful. The more successful it got, the more people were hired, and as the organisation expanded geographically, he started to become overstretched – "he couldn't be present in the same way" (which is a good example of why issues with control need to be examined early on in a leader's inner transformation work). As he had disempowered his top team and they became yes-men, the organisation "lost its operational rudder... [and eventually] it drove the business into the ground."

Leading with fear and coercion in the UK and other similar countries is no longer an acceptable cultural norm, especially in a buoyant job market. It is, at best, a short-term motivating force. More often, it drives people away; if they stay, resentment builds.

No one can be perfect all the time, and I have witnessed many a Real Model slip up (including myself). After all, we are only human. However, when someone is constantly operating in False God energy, fueled by ego and overconfidence, problems will begin to arise.

People are complex, and whilst Hank had some great leadership attributes, underneath the success, there were shaky foundations. This created an overdependence on him and left the team feeling unable to act without his presence, which can be effective when the leader is present. But as the organisation scaled, his presence became diluted. This example also highlights the need for a good, balanced leadership team or Board, with the right governance structure, to act as a safeguard when the leader cannot self-regulate.

The role of a Board is to provide governance, guidance and oversight to an organisation. It does not manage the operational aspects of a business – that responsibility lies with the CEO and their leadership team. However, ultimately, the buck does stop with the Board.

The Great Recession of 2007–2009 is still etched in the memories of many executives. It was cited as the worst global economic downturn since the Great Depression of 1929–1939. Several wrongdoings in the financial sector resulted in the collapse of the housing market. A key root cause of this is widely regarded as weak governance. Boards of financial companies were criticised for lacking the understanding, data and independence needed to fulfil their roles. Meanwhile, operationally, CEOs were under pressure to hit financial metrics with very few checks in place, and many undertook risky behaviour to hit them.

In the UK prior to that period, Fred Goodwin – also known as Fred the Shred due to his aggressive cost-cutting – was the CEO of the Royal Bank of Scotland (RBS). His vision and strategy were to transform RBS into one of the world's largest banks. At its peak, RBS had a balance sheet of £2.2 trillion, making it, at one point, the largest bank in the world by assets. It employed 226,000 people.

In 2007, RBS led a consortium, alongside Fortis and Banco Santander, in a hostile takeover of ABN AMRO. The deal was worth £55 billion and, at the time, was the largest banking takeover in history.

As the world was beginning to wake up to the unfolding economic downturn, RBS found itself overleveraged. Neither bank entered the deal from a position of financial strength, and the timing could not have been worse, with early warning signs already emerging in the financial markets. It is now widely regarded as one of the worst deals in banking history.

A year later, post-merger, RBS was bleeding cash. As its share price collapsed, the UK government was forced to step in with a £45.5 billion bailout – one of the largest in history. Fred Goodwin had to step down as CEO under intense criticism.

As mentioned above, governance failure was considered a root cause. The Board, chaired at the time by Sir Tom McKillop, had unanimously agreed to the ABN AMRO deal. They were widely criticised for failing in their duties to provide oversight, placing too much trust in the CEO, and lacking the necessary financial expertise. Later on, several Board members either resigned or were replaced, as a Board refresh was one of the conditions attached to the UK government's bailout.

Despite the size of the takeover, no regulator intervened at the time. They later had to review their own failures and publicly admit their shortcomings.

Fred Goodwin became a symbol of the worst-case scenario of ego run amok. Personally, he was stripped of his knighthood, but avoided bankruptcy, criminal actions and kept an estimated £16 million pension. Today, there is little public information available about him; he appears to have withdrawn from public life.

The case above is a powerful example of ego and leadership, and the scale of damage a False God can create – even with governance structures, a Board and regulators in place. When those checks and balances are not robust enough, the consequences can be catastrophic.

A False God represents pure ego and overconfidence, which will inevitably lead to problems in the fullness of time. A Real Model may also display an excess of ego at times, but they must find ways to keep grounded or have systems in place to check themselves. Ultimately, leaders are only human, but the damage they can cause can be significant. That's why it's essential to have strong and effective governance in place.

Films and TV often tell the story of someone fighting to be a leader, achieving it, and then letting it all go to their head. That's usually where the story of the False God stops, just as it did with Fred Goodwin. But the Real Model is different; they're not a competent jerk, and have a second act: a chance at redemption.[10]

If you see yourself as a Real Model, and this chapter resonates with you, then now is the time to course correct, before redemption becomes out of reach. What help can you get to manage overconfident impulses? Who or what can help you stay grounded?

Ego, Fear and Courage

Sigmund Freud is one of the most influential and foundational figures in modern psychology. He introduced the structured model of the psyche, which consists of three parts:

1. **Ego.** Rational thought, decision making, reality testing; mediates between the desire of the Id and the rules of the Superego. Largely conscious, but some parts, like defence mechanisms, operate unconsciously.

2. **Superego.** Moral, ideals, and social norms; strives for perfection; induces guilt or pride; spans both conscious and unconscious.

3. **Id.** Unconscious level; operates on the pleasure principle (immediate gratification), the drive for survival, desire and aggression.

Freud believed people are driven by a need to feel good and avoid pain, often without even realising it. Inside us, there's a constant tug-of-war between our basic urges, our sense of right and wrong and the need to stay realistic. This struggle affects everything we do, including how we lead.

As part of Freud's work, he started to develop the concept of ego strength, which is "an individual's ability to cope with stress, deal with adversity and recover from setbacks. When a person has good ego strength, they can manage the challenges that they face without resorting to harmful or unhealthy coping mechanisms."[11] It can be most widely connected to resilience, adaptability and courage. It is something that can be developed through wellbeing practices such as mindfulness, meditation and therapy. In this context, a strong ego is a good thing.

Another element of leadership that emerged in the interviews was the concept of courage. Courage is the ability to confront fear, pain and uncertainty. A Real Model or True Leader will draw upon their courage and do the right thing. There are strong links between this behaviour and leading from the front/taking a stand.

In *The Social Animal: The Hidden Sources of Love, Character, and Achievement*, David Brooks cites a Penn State study showing that while half of student surveys said they would protest if someone made a sexist comment in their presence, "so powerful is fear that even when motivated by what we consider right, most of us will not step up to the plate. Only 16% actually would. It takes real courage to speak up, to go against the social norm, to shatter norms".[12] History books are full of those who took a stand, suffered the consequences, but did it anyway.

Having the courage to speak out and doing so even when it got a person in trouble was mentioned by some in the Participant Group. This is a concept I have seen explored in simulations. For example, a group was asked, "What would you do if a client of a $10,000 million contract showed sexist behaviour, or if you were very junior and your senior boss balled out another member of staff to the point they cried?" We would all like to speak truth to power, but there are consequences.

I have done it myself, and yes, it has been career-limiting. Would I do it again? I think I would. That said, in some situations, I would have approached it differently. A few years ago, I came across the 4 D's of intervening safely, created by Dr D. Edwards. They support the idea of being an active bystander rather than a passive one. The 4 D's are:

1. **Direct:** Call out the negative behaviour in the moment

2. **Distract:** Shift the conversation

3. **Delegate:** Get someone involved if a person doesn't feel safe or able to intervene

4. **Delay:** Step away or wait for the situation to pass.

This is just a quick overview, so I have put together a more detailed guide, which can be found in the online resource centre. The link to this resource is located at the back of this book.

We all need a healthy ego, and leadership presents us with problems which involve real courage. A False God will often hide from this, or superficially talk a good game. A Real Model will try and do the right thing, but a True Leader has what I call smart courage. Don't be a martyr for a cause; be courageous in a smart way so that the situation is dealt with, and you are recognised for grace and courage under fire. This is in contrast to falling on your own sword, no matter how well-intentioned.

Confidence and Doubt

During the discussion with Participant 17, they raised an interesting point. When asked what the top three characteristics are that make a good leader, they responded, "trusting yourself, even when in doubt." It struck a powerful chord, as doubt is widely recognised as a common part of the leadership journey. But it also raises a thought-provoking question: If you doubt yourself, can you truly say you trust yourself? How does a leader maintain self-trust in the face of uncertainty? This felt particularly relevant for emerging leaders, who are often navigating an identity shift and a lack of anchoring, making the challenge even more complex.

A leader who never doubts themselves may drift into arrogance and is likely a False God. A healthy amount of doubt can actually shape and strengthen confidence. At the same time, confidence can help make doubt productive, as long as it doesn't tip into paralysis or undermine self-belief. When held in balance, doubt can act as a vital antidote to overconfidence.

There is also the consideration of a False God, who may appear arrogant, but their arrogance is a mask for doubt. These people are internally insecure, which is an unhealthy state.

This question was then introduced and explored with the wider Leadership Participant group. Leaders, it was noted, need to convey "an air of confidence" (Participant 33). Alan (Participant 35) shared that doubt acts as a "self-audit … it causes me to check in with my thinking and stay true to what we are trying to do, and to my own [and the organisation's] values." Some of the greatest leaders have experienced deep periods of doubt, even those who won't admit it. In contrast, an unchecked ego can be very dangerous.

Doubt, however, needs to remain within healthy bounds. As Participant 27 put it, if your doubts become so overwhelming that they erode your confidence, you need to find a way to "snap out of it." The advice shared was clear: If a leader finds themselves living too much in doubt, don't let it trip you up. And if it is, or if it looks like it might be, seek help. Reach out to a trusted confidant, manager, or mentor/coach. Talk it through, game out scenarios and voice your concerns so you can work through them.

There was a general feeling that there should be room for doubt. It can be helpful by triggering other opinions and opening people up to changing their minds when presented with new facts.

Organisational culture and norms need to be considered if a leader openly expresses doubt. Publicly and openly questioning oneself can create perception issues around their capability. Most of us would agree that we can sense fear and doubt, and it can be infectious.

If doubt is exhibited at the wrong time and in the wrong way, then it can negatively affect staff morale, productivity and even lead to higher attrition. It can also impact how a company is perceived during analyst calls and could contribute to stock price volatility. As we've seen before, CEOs often operate under a relentless spotlight.

This can be addressed by using more strategic language (please see my article on this topic in the resources hub for more information). Additionally, rephrase areas of doubt as points of discussion, fact-gathering, or promoting collaborative knowledge-sharing.

When interviewing Alan, I found the self-audit point such a great way of looking at things. It was a remarkably positive approach to turning what could have been a negative frame of reference into something beneficial. Below are some questions you could use when doing a self-audit.

1. Identify doubt. How is it showing up in your body? Notice your shoulders, stomach and clenched jaw. Then ask yourself, when did this last happen? Is this triggering something else?

2. What specific area do you have doubts?

3. What are you doubting: the person or the situation? Try to apply situational awareness – which factors are okay and which ones are not.

4. How are your confidence levels? Does this fit as a core or situational problem?

5. If this is rooted in newly emerging leadership status, can you reach out to a manager, mentor, coach, or more experienced friend who might have navigated this before?

6. Have you got the time to work this through? If not, try to hold the line. Create a pause or a holding position: something like, "That's a really interesting point. I'll need to think on that and come back to you."

7. Ask yourself if you're reacting to this with "overs": overconfidence, being overly responsible, over-explaining, or over-thinking. What is the "overs" filling a gap for? And, what tools do you normally have in place to stop this?

8. Ask yourself if in a year's time: Will this be an issue?

9. The best bit of advice I was once given was, "It's only a problem if it's an actual problem. Most of the time, it is just a thing that needs a solution. You may not like the solution, but it is a solution nonetheless."

10. Time box it.

As an emerging leader, you must have some level of trust in yourself to even start your leadership journey. As you continue down this path, your relationship with trust will be challenged. It's not great, but it does help with growing into becoming a more experienced emerging leader. Doubt can be a great self-audit; using it as a personal inquiry is a powerful tool. This is how a True Leader hones their critical thinking skills, makes the best decisions they can at the time and has a great and trusting relationship with themselves (and in some cases a better night's sleep).

Workthenticity®: A Realistic Approach to "Authenticity" at Work

The concept of authenticity at work has gained significant attention in recent years, especially in discussions about leadership. Yet, what does authenticity truly mean in the workplace? Are we ever genuinely authentic, or are we simply presenting variations of ourselves tailored to different social contexts? For instance, the self we project with friends, family, or colleagues will be similar but different. This fluidity is natural and necessary, as each environment demands a different set of behaviours, attitudes and emotional tones, like in the segment above on how and when leaders exhibit doubt.

Leadership adds an even more complex layer to this dynamic. Leaders are expected to embody strength, calmness and assurance for their teams. Employees look to their leaders for stability, particularly in times of uncertainty. If a leader were to act entirely "authentic" in moments of stress, revealing unfiltered fear or vulnerability, it could destabilise the team (as shared above). Authenticity in leadership often means balancing honesty with an awareness of the cultural landscape, the issue at hand, the people involved, and the responsibility to maintain morale while delivering on strategy.

As such, I coined the term "workthentic®," which encapsulates a pragmatic balance of being authentic at work, while also being mindful that it occurs within a professional setting. Much like how we adapt our behaviour to meet the needs of a grandparent at Sunday dinner, we adapt at work to reflect respect for the environment and the individuals within it. Workthenticity® recognises that a person brings a version of themselves to work that aligns with professional expectations, while still retaining core personal values. This approach is neither disingenuous nor entirely unfiltered; it is an intentional effort to show up in the best and most appropriate way.

Research supports this nuanced view. Psychologists argue that authenticity is not about rigidly adhering to one's "true self" but about aligning one's actions with values across contexts. A 2011 study by Gino, Kouchaki and Galinsky found that people who adapt their behaviours to different situations while staying grounded in their core principles are perceived as more authentic by others.

In essence, workthenticity® challenges the notion of authenticity vs. inauthenticity. It acknowledges the practical realities of work while encouraging individuals to reflect on their values in ways that uplift and support a working environment. Leaders, in particular, should embrace workthenticity®, ensuring their actions inspire trust and stability without compromising their humanity and their soul.

This subject was explored tangentially in the research carried out for this book, around leadership and being vulnerable. Various scenarios were explored. All agreed that a certain measure of vulnerability is acceptable.

Participant 9 shared that he would not trust a leader who didn't show some level of vulnerability.

A few cited examples in their industries of leaders who had been openly vulnerable, and they admired the leaders for doing so. Some Participants said that they had opened up about physical and mental health areas where they felt vulnerable. When they shared their stories with others, they found that people really supported them and were positively receptive to what they shared.

Participant 18 said their organisation has a session on the importance of being vulnerable in their management training.

Participant 12 discussed the benefits of opening up with a small circle of trusted people versus sharing with everyone. This might be better for those where the organisational culture will not support this type of leadership (as mentioned in the segment above).

A debate arose over whether vulnerability is perceived as a weakness or as an opportunity to tap into an inner, empowering strength. Those involved in this discussion agreed it was, and it made them better people and leaders. Participants 3 and 31 highlighted the fact that vulnerability is not the same as being weak. However, some organisational cultures do confuse the two.

The False God's invincibility did not seem authentic. The feedback was that leaders are human, and "showing vulnerability makes you relatable" (Participant 2). Through the practice of being workthentic®, vulnerabilities can be shared in a strategic, honest, meaningful and mindful way.

As this is a new area, it requires new professional skills to ground yourself workthentically. This is something U-G-U, my coaching business, has done a lot of work on. For more information, please go to the Resources Hub.

Summary

This chapter started with René Descartes' famous quote, "I think, therefore I am." Whilst I am not asking aspiring or emerging leaders to practice existentialism, you must believe that you are a leader. However, thinking alone does not make it so. Leadership is not simply assumed; it is forged, granted and is constantly evolving. Moving from management into leadership is not just a change in job title; it is a shift in identity, requiring emotional labour, vulnerability and courage. That being said, don't wait for the job title; start emerging into leadership.

Emerging leaders face a philosophical and real-world battle: the idealised inner vision of leadership that clashes with the ambiguity and complexity of real leadership. Research suggests this identity shift takes 12–18 months and is anything but linear. Leaders must navigate ambiguity, doubt, imposter syndrome (both real and perceived), ego, and the temptation to revert to what helped contribute to their success as managers: control, taking action, and perfectionism, among other things.

Where once there was certainty and expertise, now there is responsibility, ambiguity and the need to let go. There is no room to hold on to old wounds and frameworks. Leadership demands moving from control to trust, from doing to enabling and empowering, from output to impact.

True leadership isn't about flawless execution; it's about creating the conditions for others to thrive. It's about shaping systems, strategies, culture and people, whilst becoming more visible.

Emerging leaders often struggle with internal conflicts: feelings of being an "imposter" arise because their identity is still evolving, and sometimes because teams initially treat new leaders as outsiders. They must navigate group rituals, relationship-building, and gradual acceptance, all while managing the immense emotional and cognitive load of learning a new way of being.

This is the first chapter that acknowledges the blurred lines between the archetypes. Every Real Model has a bit of False God, and some False Gods will have a bit of a Real Model. A True Leader accepts they will not always be a Real Model and is aware of their False God tendencies. They will do the raw internal work. Integrity serves as a compass, and doubt acts as a self-audit. Ego must be checked before it corrupts. Smart courage is part of the make-up of a True Leader. They will not blindly go out and fight every fight, but will take a stand and do what is right, using strategic tools.

This chapter also examines the power and danger of the ego. All leaders have an ego, but it is the management of that ego that defines how a True Leader can balance the Real Model and False God within.

Stories like that of Anamina (a recovering perfectionist) and Hank (someone who initially achieved an ego-driven success, but followed by collapse) reveal how unchecked ego, poor governance and leader-centric models can be organisationally catastrophic. However, this must not be confused with ego strength, which is a mark of resilience, adaptability, and courage.

Confidence and doubt are explored not as opposites, but as partners in a healthy leadership psyche. True leaders leave space for self-questioning without allowing it to paralyse them. They practice what I call "workthenticity"®: a grounded authenticity adapted to the needs of a professional work setting, while remaining aligned to their core values. Vulnerability, when used mindfully, can create connection and trust rather than undermine leadership presence.

From an organisational perspective, all leaders – False Gods more so – need strong governance structures. Boards and oversight bodies should not aim to control leaders but proportionally support and check them.

Reflections and Actions

- Appropriate, pragmatic and proportional is an emerging leader's friend. This is the shield to your sword, your safety net.

- Encourage real governance, not just formal governance, to be in place: strong, independent checks and balances are essential. These do not have to be to the detriment of doing business.

- If something is wrong, a person shouldn't have to summon extra courage to call it out – that suggests a number of cultural problems are festering beneath the surface. Whistleblowing training should be presented in the form of case studies and learning lessons, while also encouraging and praising the courage to speak up.

- Stop advocating authenticity; workthenticity® should be the preference. There may be the odd company that truly wants this, but in general, that is not the case.

- Leadership is not a title but an evolving identity. Embrace the inner transformation journey. If this chapter resonates, be prepared for a raw experience that will help you break free from old habits and frameworks. When you get to that point, it is such a freeing feeling!

- Recognise the emotional labour in the journey: imposter syndrome, doubt and ego-management are normal parts of leadership growth.

- When confronting what needs to be addressed, do so when it is right and ensure that you do it strategically.

- Be mindful of how to transition from expert to enabler. Practise smart courage.

Chapter Five

Leadership Realities

"I am comfortable with my mess."
– Carole Epee

This chapter examines the challenges faced by emerging leaders who have progressed beyond the initial trials and tribulations of their first 12 – 18 months in a leadership role. Emerging leaders grow in experience and will have navigated their way out of some challenging situations, perhaps sustained the odd "corporate bruise" here and there. As Participant 4 says, "Everyone has their battleground fight." They are thinking strategically, tactically and are empowering their followers, not just doing.

As they develop their leadership identity mid-way through and onwards, emerging leaders must keep these strategic considerations in mind as they consider how to shape their leadership and any legacy they may want to leave. This period will include winning, losing and playing the long game, sometimes to the detriment of their reputation in the short term. This way, they're able to prioritise several fires and not just react to every emergency.

Emerging leaders need to be strategic in what opportunities they take on. The challenges are bigger, and the stakes higher. We all know what happened to those who accepted the Trojan horse! Not every opportunity is a step forward; some are invitations to fail gracefully for others.

The Emerging Leadership Journey: Closer to the Finish Line

A big part of an emerging leader's journey comes from learning and building expertise. Anecdotally, it takes 1 year to learn (expect a wobble at 3–4 months. If after 6 months it isn't right for you, look elsewhere), 2 years to get good at something, and 5–10 years to become an expert. This aligns with Malcom Gladwell, who mentioned in his book *Outliers* that 10,000 hours/10 years is required to achieve expert performance.

As all leaders progress, certain pathways will be followed. A Real Model/True Leader will endeavour to be the best leader they can be. They won't necessarily aim for mastery, but will constantly work to improve. A False God will not think they need this and will carry on. I have observed five trends in this area:

1. Entrepreneurs will pick their own path and gain mastery in their chosen area(s).

2. False Gods chase status by relying more on political acumen than on any proper and deep knowledge acquisition to progress. They ignore deep learning or find no need for it, as they have already "learnt from the school of life."

3. Real Model often experience gradual promotions and are committed to continuous learning. A variation of this is the Exceptional Achiever, an outlier with a strong drive for knowledge acquisition, high early performance and excellent emotional intelligence (EI), and whose progression is often fast-tracked.

4. When a Real Model (a competent leader) is intentionally or unintentionally put in a position to fail, and doesn't have the necessary support, the experience may offer valuable life lessons and drive future learning. However, it can also be so painful that it stunts any further mastery or progression from a promotional perspective.

5. The Peter principle comes from the work of Dr. Laurence J. Peter, who posits that individuals in organisations can be promoted to the point of their "level of incompetence."[1] In essence, they keep being promoted until they are so far away from their competency, they become incompetent. Often, they are seat warmers and avoid enough trouble to warrant being sacked. They do not possess the requisite mastery to perform the job for which they are hired.

From a tenure perspective, leaders in scenarios 2 and 5 tend to be those who move frequently and have short tenures, which is why competency-based interviews and due diligence are crucial when hiring at this level.

Some Real Models are able and do want to follow a more traditional progression, obtaining mastery as they go.

The Managing Director (MD) level or Business Unit Head level tenure tends to range between 3–5 years on average, per role, with C-Suite being slightly longer, around 5–7 years on average, per role. There are several pull factors – such as promotion, increased influence or control, better compensation, stronger alignment with personal values, or simply a desire to change – and push factors, including poor performance (which accounts for approximately 10% of CEO movements), strategic misalignment (such as during mergers and acquisitions), cultural fit or burn out, that influence why leaders move. Post-COVID-19 tenure data suggest movements are becoming more frequent. A recent cultural trend which may help explain this is the Great Resignation, where, post-COVID-19, people re-evaluated their life priorities and moved into new roles that offered better work/life balance, increased flexibility and personal fulfilment.

Therefore, the level of mastery a new MD has achieved is critical because many move on before obtaining full mastery. That's why the emerging leader period is so important; it serves as their core learning group. This could help explain why some leaders lose their jobs quite quickly: They did not have the chance to develop, like the Peters of this world.

There are some leaders who move around more frequently. It could be the case of an Exceptional Achiever progressing rapidly, or an underperformer avoiding performance management or jumping before being fired. On the other hand, some remain in their roles for decades. But is a longer tenure a good thing? Research suggests that staying in the same leadership role for more than 7.6 years can be considered the upper limit of an effective tenure. Beyond that, there is a risk of stagnation, complacency, institutionalism, lack of innovation and, even with teams, groupthink.[2] Some of the participants from the experienced group talked about strategic movements and the benefits of being pulled into a role, rather than pushed. At the time of hiring, the right candidate is typically brought in with a strategic objective that goes beyond business as usual. It is important that they have a solid grounding or the right support to make the role a success for them and others. For example, a wartime manager may be best suited for periods of crisis, because they might need to turn around an underperforming business, for instance.

It is not uncommon for a "golden handshake" to be offered in what is known as a "dead man/woman walking" position. In such cases, a leader may be expected to take the fall or hold the line during a transition period, often with the promise of additional benefits or compensation. They are usually aware of the possible risk of not having a future beyond that appointment at the organisation, and potentially a tarnished reputation. However, some may view taking on this type of role as an act of courage, and with the right positioning, their reputation may be able to survive the initial storm.

Challenging Role Questions

1. Do your due diligence on the written and unwritten cultural norms, your direct manager, and the team you are going into. Look at the risks and opportunities, as well as your threats and vulnerabilities. Can you actually do the job? Don't think that you need to know everything, as there will always be stretch areas. But do you have the foundational mastery to do it and/ or the support to get there?

2. Go in with a clear awareness of the *real* ask (refer to glass cliff considerations below). If it is a risk and you still want to proceed, make sure you have the right protections and appropriate remuneration in place.

3. Crisis and burnout are risks to any leader, especially in problematic roles. So think about what is reasonable for you from a time and energy perspective. If you do a 50-hour week at 100%, you are already operating at full capacity. Consider what can happen on a bad day or during a difficult period (not even a worst-case scenario). You'll need to add an extra 30% buffer for energy, time and capacity. That is the baseline for your role. If you're already at 100% and haven't factored in the buffer, it will catch up with you. And if the challenge turns out to be a marathon problem, not a sprint, burnout is almost inevitable. It can kill!

4. Timebox the role with a bit of flexibility and have an exit plan. Understand the timeline of your tenure and when to start exploring new opportunities. The time frame on job searches at this level, usually involving a specialist recruitment agency or head-hunter, is around 18–12 months. Some senior leadership positions will have a year's notice, and negotiations are not done quickly.

5. If you have a six-month notice, be mindful that your sphere of control and power will start to diminish. This could mean emails won't be responded to as quickly as they were, some people will bump you to the bottom of their catch-up pile, dinners and drinks will become late-morning coffees, and no new projects will come your way (or a flurry of urgents will

load up your day). This will be another identity shift, but consider how you can create space to transition into the next role or chapter during that time frame. The only time the above will not happen is if you are transitioning into a more senior role within the same organisation or are not competing with an industry peer.

6. If you do this role, do you have the financial resources in place to find the next role? This is because the process can take six months to a year. If you don't, consider what clauses or benefits you want in your contract to make sure you have the right protections in place.

At least with a challenging role, there is a chance. The "glass cliff" concept is similar to this, but slightly different, as it involves a leader with a minority-type characteristic – for example, a woman – being promoted into a role or asked to run a risky project during a time of crisis, where the risk of failure is high.[3] This is not always done with conscious awareness on the part of the emerging leader.

The term was coined by Michelle Ryan and Alex Haslam, who analysed FTSE 100 companies and found that women were more likely to be appointed to board positions after an organisation had suffered negative financial impact as seen in stock performance, whereas men were appointed more frequently after periods of stability. This trend has been noted in other studies, across industries and geographies.

"In times of crisis, leaders – no matter who they are – tend to be seen as ineffective and part of the problem. When the leader is an occupational minority, any failure or lack of improvement tends to be attributed to their personal failings rather than to the situation. In a phenomenon called the saviour effect, the minority leader is then replaced by a more demographically typical leader who 'saves the day.' This both perpetuates leadership stereotypes in the organisation and constricts diverse candidates' future opportunities."[4]

And it is not just in the boardroom. There are many so-called "wonderful opportunity" projects, pitched to ambitious emerging leaders wanting to prove themselves, where they are not set up for success.

Ways to Spot These Types of Situations

1. Consider why *you* specifically have been hired (now is not the time to be overconfident or overly humble), especially if there was a more suitable internal candidate. If there is, ask yourself: Why did they not de-risk the situation by employing a known emerging leader versus a new one who would lack internal organisational knowledge, and would need time acclimatising and building a network?

2. Are you being paid more than the market rate for this role? Not quite danger money, but still better than the average. Why?

3. Look for fatal flaws. Is it winnable? Not *could* you win, but *realistically*, is it winnable? As Sun Tzu said, "Intense effort cannot overcome fatal flaws [and where there are flaws, such as a lack of resources] ... "a slow death is death nonetheless."[5]

When Marissa Mayer was at Google, she had a profile of brilliance: She was an ambitious, data-driven and highly sought-after technologist.

At the time of her appointment as Chief Executive Officer (CEO) of Yahoo, she was 37 and pregnant. Being female, she was included in only 4.2% of female CEOs in the Fortune 500. She was its CEO from 2012 to 2017. She had stepped into the role following five CEOs in five years. At the time, Yahoo was losing market share, had internal problems, a dysfunctional operating model and had missed innovation opportunities to invent and innovate.

Her tenure received mixed feedback. For example, Yahoo acquired Tumblr for USD 1.1 billion in 2013 but ultimately sold it in 2017 for around USD 3 million – a 98% loss. In 2016, Yahoo experienced two of the largest data breaches in history, affecting over three billion users. As a result, she and others were required to testify before a US Senate Committee.

As CEO and a public figure, appearing in female leadership rankings, receiving Women of the Year awards and even gracing the cover of Vogue, she was highly visible, as reflected in her online presence and the level of exposure she received in that period.

During her tenure, there were boardroom changes, activist shareholder pressure, and legal disputes, all of which likely compounded issues, although they may have served as some form of check and balance. Her tenure ended in 2017 when Verizon acquired some of Yahoo's assets. She resigned with a rumoured $23 million termination package. Professionally, she went on to take up other board roles and investments and founded Sunshine.

There was no direct successor as CEO of Yahoo, as the company effectively ceased to exist as an independent entity. The successor of the combined organisation was Tim Armstrong.

The above situation is widely regarded as a textbook example of the glass cliff: She was brought in to rescue a collapsing company, judged harshly in a no-win situation, and exited with much of the failure pinned on her – despite complex, pre-existing challenges.

Whilst some of the above reflect situations being done *to* a leader, they, of course, have a choice in how they navigate these challenging situations. Some leaders I have worked with over the years have tried to excuse bad behaviour with "I've been brought in to be the bastard/ bitch," which tends to align with the False God type of leader.

As leaders complete their tenure successfully, they ask themselves, "What is next?" In the Leadership Participant group, most at the managing director or CEO level had already started to plan next steps, such as monetising a hobby or passion, progressing into NED roles, consulting/coaching or even just putting in place financial plans for retirement. Although it didn't come up in the group, some next chapters for leaders could also involve teaching, public service or focusing on social goals.

What the experienced group all had in common was that they knew what was next, had thought about it and had already started making plans. This was different from the emerging leaders, as some members of the group were still in an exploratory mode. I would suggest that an emerging leader at this stage think very strategically. Where are you going, and what do you need in place to help you reach your destination? Start considering how you see the end of your tenure playing out now. There are some mentees or coachees who know in their early twenties that they want the C-Suite. There are a number of moves that need to happen to get there. If someone nearing the end of their emerging leader journey decides they want C-Suite, you will be competing with people who have been planning, building the network and gaining the experience and expertise. This is incredibly hard to beat. If it is a hard no, then fine; but if you're unsure, then start making the right moves, such as executive sponsorship, stretch projects or secondments, so that you have the option to take them if you want later on.

The Myth of a Working Week and Work-Life Balance

Time is arguably the most precious resource a person has. There is often a view that being a leader involves a larger chunk of time than that expended by the average worker.

Anecdotally, a 5-day/40-hour workweek became the norm. Henry Ford implemented the 8-hour workday in 1914.

One of the driving forces behind Henry Ford's thinking was optimum productivity. However, studies show that productivity wanes after 4-6 hours of focused work. Also, the 9–5 window doesn't work for all, and some people tend to be more productive earlier or later in the day. In essence, flexibility cannot only boost productivity, but research shows it can also benefit employee satisfaction.

Whilst hybrid working has been around for decades, it became more of a norm due to COVID-19 (with some companies trying to revert to pre-COVID-19 practices). For those able to take it up, it offered far greater flexibility.

Whilst data varies for leaders and there are many factors to consider, estimates suggest they work anywhere between 50 and 120 hours per week. In their research, Sylvia Ann Hewlett and Carolyn Buck Luce found that "workers who hold what we consider extreme jobs (a designation based on responsibilities and other attributes beyond pay), the hours are even more punishing. Most of them (56%) work 70 hours or more a week, and 9% work 100 hours or more."[6] Long working hours are linked to both psychological and physical consequences – including heightened stress, cardiovascular issues, and mental health challenges.

Another cultural trend which may be challenging the "work too hard" ethos is the rise of the four-day working week trials. These have been conducted in various countries, with mostly positive outcomes. In 2022, the UK conducted the largest trial to date, involving 61 companies and around 2,900 employees. The results showed a 35% average increase in revenue, a 57% decrease in attrition, and a 71% decrease in employee burnout.

Geographical cultural norms do impact approaches to work-life balance. Western societies often glorify "hustle culture," while Scandinavian countries prioritise work-life harmony. In Japan, the term "karoshi" – meaning "death from overwork" – underscores the dangers of excessive work, with some reported deaths involving people who have worked 80–100+ hour workweeks. In 1993, the EU rolled out the Working Time Directive, which aimed to limit the average working week to 48 hours and to protect workers' health and promote fair work practices. It has not gone without challenge. For example, the UK opted out of the directive (now a moot point).

Work-life balance boosts job satisfaction, retention and overall morale. This also impacts an organisation positively by having a healthier and more productive workforce, and lower instances of health problems. From a purely commercial point, it could lower insurance premiums, reduce spending on employee benefits, fewer claims, not to mention the upside of good productivity and less absenteeism. Some organisations are using it as a talent attraction and retention model. Having the best talent is not only a differentiator competitively, but can also mean better quality products, a higher rate of innovation and employee satisfaction, all of which translate into superior financial performance.

If a rigid five-day working week is not productive, no one wants to do it, and organisations recognise the benefits of more flexible ways of working, why are they not breaking from the historical cultural norm? Or are they? This area was explored with the Leadership Participant group.

The question posed was "Do you work more than 50 hours regularly?" There was no correlation with age, DE&I markers or experience around working more/less. But 70% said they work more than 50 hours, which answers the initial question: Do leaders work longer than the average worker? The answer is yes.

Participants in the more experienced group were comfortable in setting and enforcing boundaries with themselves and their organisations.

Participant 15 shared that she is "very strict with time and boundaries. Creating boundaries is really important. I make sure I focus on things I should be focusing on. Sometimes it is difficult. Just because you like doing it, doesn't mean you should be doing it."

An emerging leader should expect to work more than the average working week. Where this approach tends to work well is when a boss expects extra effort to be put in when needed, but is equally comfortable with the emerging leader taking shorter days, longer breaks or additional time off when that extra effort isn't required.

This is where a Real Model can learn from a False God; you'll never catch them doing more than they need to (and sometimes not even that). Focus on what's impactful and necessary. If it isn't, then why are you doing it? The True Leader gets this balance right.

Navigating Office Politics: A Real-World Hunger Games

The Hunger Games is a popular series of books written by Suzanne Collins, which were made into films starring Jennifer Lawrence, Liam Hemsworth and Lenny Kravitz, among others. The story follows a young lady called Katniss Everdeen, growing up in a future dystopian society where children or young adults have to compete to the death in a televised survival competition. This type of competition is a tool for oppression, and the involvement of Katniss triggers a fight for justice and a better world. Undertones in the book are around negative politics such as propaganda, manipulation, power struggles and clashes, which bring out the best and worst of people.

Politics is just a way to govern; it is neither good nor bad. John F. Kennedy once said, "Politics is the price we pay to live in a free world." Despite the good that it does and can do, it often evokes negative connotations. Even the impartial Cambridge Dictionary leans towards the negative on office politics, reducing it to "the relationships within an organisation that allow particular people to have power over others."[7] However, they are not wrong.

Not all cultures are ruthlessly political, but some can be. "Research indicates that office politics is more prevalent in larger organisations and tends to be more pronounced in competitive industries such as finance, law, and politics."[8] The corporate world is considered political in nature, particularly at the top table of power. Numerous books and films depict it as a type of battlefield characterised by intense competition, power struggles, betrayal and political manoeuvring.

For many leaders, the demands of the day-to-day are challenging enough. But the additional layer of constant political machinations and rivalries often makes the experience far more taxing, requiring more emotional labour from its "contestants."

Over the years, numerous professionals have reported instances of being undermined, sabotaged or outright attacked by colleagues vying for their position. Adecco, a UK recruiter, found that a third of UK workers "cite office politics as a major contributing factor to feelings of unhappiness in the workplace …. [leaving] 29% of UK workers spending every Sunday dreading the coming working week."[9] Work done since the study found that this figure increases with companies employing over 1,000 – it goes up to 85%. The unfortunate reality is that, in many organisations, this *is* the case. The dynamics at play can be surprisingly similar to those depicted in *The Hunger Games.*

Those inciting it are forcing people into a zero-sum game, often against the other person's will, employing tactics such as credit stealing, scapegoating, metaphorically tripping someone up, character assassinations, manipulation, prolonged campaign of microaggressions, undermining trust, all-out subversive bullying, etc.[10]

Like *The Hunger Games*, it is a fight to the death (of someone's career or role), for the other to take what they want. Whilst other options are viable, the instigator prefers the zero-sum game (usually they are overly competitive, but not necessarily loudly).

Whilst the False God may chalk these games up to survival of the fittest, there is an element of that. In reality, if the two parties, let's say Jack (instigator) and Emma were competing on a level playing field, Emma would outperform Jack. Jack, being aware and fearful of this, realises he needs to stack the deck in his favour, usually using unethical means or a few tactics from the False God playbook. And, because Jack is practised at this, to the winner go the spoils. The mistake being made here is that leaders look at the contestants in the game and congratulate the "winner." They then expect someone skilled at gaming, and assume this translates to them being effective in the actual role of being a leader. If they were, they wouldn't have had to resort to this type of game-playing in the first place. However, this isn't even faux-leadership; it isn't any type of leadership at all, just a sub-par employee being opportunistic.

Many professionals equate career success with climbing the corporate ladder, which naturally creates an atmosphere where individuals are vying for a limited number of top roles. This perceived scarcity of opportunities can lead to an intense focus on outperforming or other less ethical means. Much like the contestants in *The Hunger Games*, employees in such environments are often pitted against one another, either directly or indirectly, as they vie for survival – or in this case, career advancement.

Steve Jobs is a household name, leading companies such as Apple and Pixar. In the 1980s, a power struggle arose between him and John Sculley. Jobs had brought Scully in as Apple's CEO in 1983. Despite initially getting along well, tensions began to rise over strategy and behaviour.

Jobs attempted a boardroom coup in 1985 to remove Scully. Scully found out and compelled the board to side with him and essentially forced Jobs out.

Jobs went on to find NeXT, which, in a twist of fate, was acquired by Apple in 1997. Scully remained in situ until 1993 but was ousted after Apple lost its way without Jobs. Due to the political manoeuvring and dramatic outcomes, it has been made the subject of films and documentaries. This is an example of office politics being played out, the zero-sum game mentality in its glory, and that fact, whilst Jobs was problematic, removing such a valuable person, or "asset," did Apple a huge disservice. It is widely regarded as not having found its feet again until Jobs' return.

At its core, the corporate environment is often a system built on ambition and competition, which by themselves are not inherently bad; both can bring out the best and worst in people. However, it is when people use nefarious means, such as burning an organisational asset, that a supporter of a "survival of the fittest" mentality should consider the instigator's judgement, personal motivation and why they might dispose of – at the risk of sounding cold – a valuable asset.

While individual ambition plays a significant role in fostering corporate rivalries, the broader culture of an organisation often determines how far such behaviours can go. Toxic work environments where self-serving behaviour is rewarded create fertile ground for backstabbing and manipulation. Conversely, organisations with strong or positive governance, transparent processes and a culture of collaboration are less likely to experience such dysfunction. If a leader is collaborative, transparent and not skilled in this arena, then they may want to consider whether a *Hunger Games*-type organisation is the best fit for them. Equally, someone who chooses zero-sum games and is politically savvy will also not do well in a collaborative and transparent culture, where aggressive game playing is not tolerated. Jeffrey Pfeffer, the author of *The Leadership BS*, explores how the type of leadership qualities held up as good, such as authenticity and humility, are not always the traits that actually help leaders progress. He notes that organisational systems reward aggressive behaviour, creating a cycle where political tactics become necessary for survival.

For those nearing or are at the top of an organisation, navigating these challenges requires a blend of strategic thinking, EI, situational awareness and resilience. Building genuine relationships based on trust can act as a counterbalance to political games, providing a support system in difficult times. Aligning one's actions with core values and focusing on integrity can help maintain credibility, even in the face of intense rivalry.

The experiences of Katniss Everdeen in *The Hunger Games* offer a hyperbolic metaphor. Her survival hinged not only on her skills and situational awareness but also on her ability to form genuine connections and stay true to her principles. Leaders can adopt a similar approach by balancing strategic manoeuvring with a commitment to fairness and collaboration. Furthermore, mentorship and strong allies within the organisation can provide valuable guidance and advocacy. If a leader finds themselves in this situation, a coach who can offer lived experience and realistic guidance on strategically navigating these situations is crucial to success. You need to understand the players, their motivations, multiple dynamics and drivers. This means paying attention to power dynamics, how influence works and where leverage lies.

One final note: Every leader will have their failure story, often involving these types of situations. At the beginning of the book, I said, "Some of my failures have led to my biggest successes, and some of my successes have sown the seeds for my biggest failures." My biggest success then led to a similar situation to Jack's (no, I wasn't Jack) and Emma's, and it led to one of my biggest failures. It was *because* of this that I ultimately achieved a much bigger and happier success later on. But that's a story for another book!

Best of luck, these games are not the *Hunger Games*, but they are unpleasant, stressful, and not easy!

Machiavelli, Politics and Compromising Values

The promptings of this chapter came from two things:

1. Around 15 years ago, I received some training where the Leader delivering it said something that stuck with me: "The higher up you go, the more compromises you have to make." After the session, I made myself a promise: If the compromise required me to go against my values, that's as far as I'd go in that organisation.

2. A question I've found myself revisiting over the years: *Can someone effectively lead without compromising their values?* (To be clear, I'm not talking about criminal behaviour here.)

Is it naïve, vain or even arrogant to believe that your personal values should take precedence over your duty to the organisation? To believe that, on the well-worn path to leadership, *you* will be the exception, the one who never compromises and still leads at the highest level?

When it comes to advocating for going all out for what one wants, regardless of the damage, the famous quote from Niccolo Machiavelli comes to mind: "The end justifies the means." Even in Jim Collins' *Good to Great*, he says with "ferocious resolve...do whatever needs to be done to make the company great."[11] In general, the Machiavelli quote's context is often "do whatever needs to be done, without moral or ethical limitations," whereas Collins's context is around discipline, integrity and ethics. Context and leadership character are key.

Machiavelli (1469 – 1527) was a philosopher, diplomat and political theorist. *The Prince* is often regarded as one of the earliest and most influential books on political science, and remains so today. The book has been infamous over the years, being both denigrated and praised. Whilst it offers thoughts on cunning and ruthlessness, it also offers hard truths on power, perception and human nature: fundamental and basic elements of political science.

It is now widely believed that Machiavelli never actually wrote "the end justifies the means."

One of the closest interpretations comes from another of his books *Discourses on Livy*[12], where he said, "When the safety of one's country wholly depends on the resolution to be taken, no consideration of justice or injustice, humanity or cruelty, nor of glory or infamy, should be allowed to prevail." More nuanced than "the end justifies the means" as it speaks of survival, but still not a blanket statement on the end justifying the means.

Another interpretation of the phrase, believed to originate from a later translation, is "if peace and stability in all circumstances could be saved, the end justifies the means." In context, much like the Jim Collins quote, good is ultimately the end.

So, how Machiavellian was Machiavelli? It is somewhat worrying that the book, with its raw and real political theory, has been debated and guiding leaders for hundreds of years, especially since such a key and often cited passage never existed in the first place. Perhaps its popularity gave False Gods the power and tacit approval to act ruthlessly without impunity, claiming strategic political acumen and grit, when really, they were just willing to hurt others, squander valuable resources, essentially act unethically because they did not have the skill, diplomacy and patience to achieve the best outcome.

Judy Smith believes that "though we may not want to admit it, there's a "bad guy" inside all of us. All of us are capable of poor judgment and bad behaviour."[13] If that is the case, then a False God will give in to it. Even, possibly, a Real Model. In 1971, Dr Philip Zimbardo ran a now-infamous experiment called The Stanford Prison Experiment. The aim of the experiment was to see how people conform to the roles of guard and prisoner. Twenty-four male college students signed up and were assigned the role of either guard or prisoner. The study was to last for two weeks; however, it had to be terminated after six days because the guards became sexually, psychologically, and physically abusive, and the prisoners became – rightly so – emotionally distressed. This highlighted that even good people can go bad very quickly. Zimbardo later described it as the Lucifer Effect.

It comes down to a person's values. One of the questions posed to the Participant Leadership group was, "Have you, or have you seen other leaders, compromise their values?" False Gods are not going to set the right example, "some do not have great values or scruples" (Participant 7), or "they never had those [positive characteristics] values in the first place" (Participant 12).

Participant 21 shared details of a leader who had committed a criminal action. The "criminal had convinced his superiors he was brilliant at hitting his targets, but he treated his subordinates very badly. His bad behaviour had stood out to them, but not his management. On the face of it he looked like he was being successful, but that was the image being portrayed.

Participant 29 highlighted a well-known Technology leader and said that he was "successful because he has been lucky and ruthless…Being ruthless helped accelerate the amount of work done in a day, as he wasn't spending time on severance packages, worrying about people and the impact of his actions."

According to Barbara Kellerman, a thought leader in this space, "bad leadership means two things; firstly, ineffective leadership, and secondly, unethical leadership… Unethical, bad leadership can be very effective."[14] I call a leader who is politically astute but in essence a bad leader a faux-leadership, part of the False God archetype. They may be charming but only superficially, and they lack competency. But a lot can be said for knowing how to play the game.

Knowing how to play the game, in essence, is about how to understand the rules of a system and win at them. The game itself often has written and unwritten rules. A person joining a new social system, like an organisation, will be able to learn the written rules; however, the unwritten rules will only be learnt if they end up in the inner circle of power, which is usually not done from day one. Some people will be naturally better at this. For example, they are adept at reading people, strategic thinkers, possess good situational awareness and have strong social skills. This includes recognising game players. When they are playing games, they exercise diplomacy and understand power dynamics. They have had exposure to similar social systems and rules, or they are close to the base of power, which will speed things up.

Vicki McCray shared in her book *How to Swim with Sharks:* "A valuable lesson learnt… One not taught in college: Politics is present in everything you do, particularly in the workplace. The person who is successful in the workplace is not always the one who is highly educated, but the person who combines both knowledge and politics to get the job done…knowledge and political suavity that will catapult your career to a place beyond what you could ever imagine."[15]

A few points can be derived from this:

- Character is key when considering a False God and a Real Model; there can be overlap.

- Political acumen is a crucial skill, yet it is often not included in leadership training. And when it is, it is often dressed up as "influencing stakeholders," "key or ethical decision making," "managing up, down, across," and not dealing with the subject in its entirety.

- The skill alone can catapult a career despite a person's faux leadership capability.

True Leaders do the right thing even when no one is looking. They charge forward through public humiliation, even if they must stand alone and especially when others choose to retreat for personal gain.[16] Participant 3 also shared that he has lived by his personal rule: "Do what is right, not what is easy," even when it has got him into trouble. Real Models and True Leaders are not flawless, perfect or immune to pressure. They wrestle with self-doubt, understand the game's rules and ethically engage, sometimes faltering. In a world where image can often outpace substance, the enduring challenge for leaders is not just to succeed, but to do so without losing sight of the values that define them and the greater good.

Losing the Dressing Room

The higher an emerging leader ascends, the more they may have to make compromises. What that looks like is down to each emerging leader, their character and the situation at hand. Even a True Leader can make missteps, but once they are made, can they walk them back? The phrase "losing the dressing room" originates from the world of football and refers to the pivotal moment when a manager loses the trust, respect or support of his players. This breakdown in the relationship often precedes a slump in performance and, ultimately, managerial dismissal. While its origins are rooted in sport, the concept holds relevance in business and leadership. In organisational settings, it refers to the moment when leaders can no longer influence or connect with their team(s) or their followers – often with damaging consequences for morale and performance. This scenario was explored with the Leadership Participant group.

In organisations, "losing the dressing room" can take many forms.

Some don't care about having it. Participant 36 described a leader who simply didn't care whether he had the team's support. "If all you have is autocratic rule," she noted, "you're not a leader – you're a dictator." This kind of detached leadership creates disengagement at best, and sabotage at worst.

Participant 21 believes that in some cases, leaders "never had it to lose." Perhaps from this perspective, the leader either inherited toxic dynamics, walked in with damaged credibility, or relied too heavily on title over trust.

Natasha (Participant 5) shared a situation where a leader she worked with – let's call him Vlad – was not right for the role. In the end, it didn't work out, and Vlad left. A success metric, financial performance, was a lagging indicator in this scenario; revenue growth had continued, and so hitting the metrics had created an illusion of Vlad's success. It was only when senior management appeared to take a wider perspective and appreciate that the business performance was actually being constrained by Vlad that the leader in question was removed. Natasha went on to say that behind the financials, "every decision he made was the wrong one, and they started to mount up. He wasn't competent for the role, and he didn't have the respect of his leadership team or the business."

There were a few instances where leaders were leading, but had lost the dressing room and didn't realise it. Participant 31 reflected on a CEO who had once been beloved but, following a promotion and through a series of poor decisions, had become disconnected from his people. "His days are numbered," he said. "He just doesn't know he's lost it yet."

Yet not all cases end in failure. Some leaders only lose the dressing room temporarily, but manage to win it back. Some participants shared examples of leaders who admitted mistakes, took responsibility for their decisions, and re-engaged their teams through diplomacy, understanding and humility. They worked with the team to try and stop it from happening again. This aligns with the actions of a Real Model or a True Leader.

At times, emerging leaders lose the room not because they are wrong, but because the culture around them is too resistant to change. Sometimes the issue isn't the individual but the culture. If we return to the infamous Machiavelli, he warned that reforming an existing order is one of the most dangerous and difficult things a leader can do, because beneficiaries of the old system resist change, while potential beneficiaries of the new one are slow to back it. Resistance can be particularly strong when biases and group dynamics are at play.

Participant 18 recalled a workplace that frequently promoted from within, without investing in leadership training. The newly promoted individuals began with good intentions, but as their authority was tested and their lack of experience exposed, their messages "fell on deaf ears." They were not able to earn the respect of the dressing room, and certainly didn't know how to recover it.

Jenna, a mentee I worked with, opened up to me and shared how a fast-track promotion and a loss of executive sponsorship left them exposed to colleagues who resented their involvement in the leadership top team, and the changes they had implemented. They punished her through activities such as belittling, ostracising, bullying and humiliating them; "At times, they generally seemed to delight in doing it." When Jenna opened up to another female leader, the other leader implied it was a type of hazing and said it was to clip her wings. They had it done to her, and she had seen it done to other female leaders in the organisation. This was all despite the fact that the changes Jenna had implemented resulted in organisational successes and better financial and non-financial performance.

Due to the resentment she felt about being given the keys to the dressing room before her time, those who resented this took them away, and Jenna was blocked from entering the dressing room. She said that after her "wings were clipped" in a number of ways, for over a year," the male team started to let her back in, but by then the damage had been done, and she left the organisation.

Her experiences align with the experiences of people subjected to the effects of Tall Poppy Syndrome – a cultural trend where high-achieving individuals, especially women, are cut down for their success. The way it plays out in business is that female leaders are "attacked, resented, disliked, criticised, or cut down because of their achievements and/or success."[17] Sadly, this is not a rare occurrence. A study by Rumeet Billan revealed that nearly 87% of participants had experienced this type of bullying, which often leads high performers to minimise their skills, disengage and/or leave their current organisation – like Jenna did.

Losing the dressing room, then, is not always about one misstep. It can stem from a slow erosion of trust, a mismatch of values or a failure to read the room. It can result from being too inexperienced, too removed, too ambitious or too resistant to feedback. It might stem from simply being a tall poppy. From trying to initiate change. Or, resentment from others and being at the mercy of a competing power base, as well as a change in power dynamics. The longer and deeper the issues, the harder it is to turn things around. When leaders lose the dressing room, they often lose the very thing that makes leadership possible: followship.

The costs of not having or losing the dressing room are high for an emerging leader. Red flags include financial underperformance,

146

staff absenteeism, high turnover, productivity issues and cynicism surrounding communications. People only go above and beyond if remunerated, versus helping out of a spirit of organisational citizenship or negative reputational damage. It is rare to turn it around, but it can be done as seen above through humility, vulnerability and situational awareness. This will often be a positive driver, as most reasonable people will recognise it is a rare occurrence and not a professional failing.

If you don't manage to regain the dressing room, you may wish to explore options for staying or going. How will you lead if no one will follow you?

The energy and skill required to accomplish this very challenging feat will demand a lot from an emerging leader. Try and get a mentor or coach with lived experience to help you work through the multifaceted dynamics of something like this. If you do it, a seasoned leader will recognise what it took from you to undertake this type of activity; it has the hallmarks of True Leadership.

Summary

This chapter examines the challenges faced by emerging leaders who have progressed beyond the initial adjustment period and are now fully immersed in their roles. As emerging leaders mature, their perspective and actions shift from reaction to strategy, from managing fires to shaping legacy, and from technical excellence to navigating politics, values and emotional resilience.

Leadership is not a straightforward path from start to finish; it's a layered, non-linear journey that becomes messier and more complex the further an emerging leader advances. The quote at the beginning of the chapter was about an emerging leader needing to be comfortable with the mess. It is apt because at this stage, from a professional perspective, a leader has to be comfortable with the mess that is ambiguity, lack of control, and wicked decision-making in a VUCA (volatile, uncertain, complex and ambiguous) world. The inbox is never empty, the to-do list is never complete, and there are always left-field events that can take one by surprise. You would have said something in the wrong way to multiple people, possibly in a full auditorium, made some mistakes and suffered a few corporate bruises. With character, principles, a good network, holistic development and making peace with the "mess," you can then navigate this part of your world.

A core theme is the contrast between Real Models – those who lead with competence, humility and an ethical foundation – and False Gods – those who rise through politics, optics, or opportunism. The Real Model is looking for sustainability, and the False God exalts status. It is in this mess that the Real Model will struggle as they find their way through. The False God will not, as they already know the answers and arbitrarily lead until their gloss starts to fade and will often move to avoid getting found out.

Leadership roles, particularly at Managing Director or C-Suite level, are increasingly short-term, driven by both pull (opportunities) and push (burnout, misalignment) dynamics. It takes the average person decades to get to this summit, and it isn't right for everyone. Post-COVID, the landscape has accelerated; leaders are reevaluating life priorities and organisations are reassessing fit – the latter being a constant crucible of multi-generational values and culture shocks. It is questionable whether this is enough time to gain mastery in the role; establishing good foundations will ensure success.

Concepts such as the "glass cliff" and strategic placements during crisis periods – often experienced by women or minority leaders – highlight the systemic challenges many face in senior roles. These experiences are not only professionally risky but also deeply personal, requiring leaders to enter with eyes open, be strategically aware and take the necessary precautions. These can be orchestrated by False Gods, so they do not risk their own careers; they will often resort to subterfuge and nefarious tactics to entrap a naïve but hard-working Real Model.

The chapter also delves into the politics of leadership, using the hyperbolic metaphor of a real-world "Hunger Games." In many organisations, particularly large or competitive ones, leaders encounter competing agendas and/or tactical opponents. Navigating office politics becomes a survival skill – one that risks eroding an emerging leader's professional profile and self-confidence if not approached consciously.

The Machiavellian notion that "the end justifies the means" is questioned, showing how even untrue attributions to historical texts can warp leadership expectations, through poorly researched and delivered training or overly cynical coaching, capitulating to a toxic culture. Leaders must find ways to remain ethical in systems that often reward the opposite.

Leadership is not a 40-hour week; some weeks it will be more, and some weeks maybe less. Any leader struggles with boundaries, energy management and knowing when (or how) to step away. Emotional labour and burnout are very real risks – even for the most resilient.

The concept of "losing the dressing room" speaks to the erosion of trust and followship. Sometimes a leader never had it, or had access removed by other gatekeepers; some lost it due to poor judgment; often, it is a gradual disconnection – either through cultural misfit, resistance to change or the weight of cumulative missteps. In some cases, talented leaders enter organisations too early, without support and are pushed out before they have a chance to truly lead. Other times, they realise too late that they've lost the room. Yet, there are recovery stories too – where humility, vulnerability and honest re-engagement repair the bridge between leaders and teams. Based on the experience of the participant group, where a person has acted out of character and quickly tried to amend and atone, they can regain it. However, the type of misdeed coupled with actions in the aftermath can mean it is not recoverable.

Leadership is not about a perfectly polished and flawless execution. It is about intention, awareness and the smart courage to choose the hard right over the easy wrong. True leaders are not immune to failure – but they do not shy away from it, nor do they compromise their core values for momentary wins. In an era of public visibility, political tension and organisational volatility, the call is not to be perfect, but to be real, workthentic, resilient and ethically grounded.

Reflections and Actions

- Probe not just performance but also patterns. Look for frequent movement, political manoeuvring or reputational red flags when hiring for your team. For example, has a person moved on quickly in roles, or have they had fairly similar roles with slight progression and then jumped a few rungs into a "Director" role? Sometimes people talk themselves up, but that has come from a place of well-intentioned overconfidence. And before you know it, you won't have a Director *in situ* to help with your workload, but a more junior member of staff who, instead of lessening your load, will increase it and demand more of your time coaching them.

- Prioritise psychological safety and values alignment.

- Start thinking now about your "next chapter" and what legacy you want to leave.

- Crisis and burnout are risks to any leader; think about what is reasonable. Consider how much time you would typically spend on a day. And on a bad day, add an extra 30% buffer for energy, time drain, etc. That is the baseline for your next role. If you're already operating at 100% with no buffer, it will catch up with you — and if the problem turns out to be a marathon rather than a sprint, burnout is almost inevitable.

- If you're faced with a glass cliff situation, refer to the above questions in the chapter.

- Hire your personal board: This concept has been built up for the last few years. Essentially, as a business has a Board of Directors, one should have a personal board of mentors, coaches, gatekeepers and wise advisers to help support. This group is a collective that can help guide and work through challenges, such as how to gain back the respect of the dressing room, or maybe advise you when it is beyond repair. Any emerging leader should put one together early on. Each member will bring a unique skill to help support, e.g. a well-known wicked decision maker, a coach on executive presence or a gatekeeper to the executive team you want to become more visible to. As the leader evolves, old goals are met and new ones are identified – so it's essential to "induct" new board members and gracefully roll off those who helped achieve the earlier goals.

- Maintain situational awareness, monitor power dynamics and consciously decide how you might wish to respond. Each level will have its own politics and dynamics, management team, leadership and C-Suite. Often, the root cause of political moves will stem from something going on at the top table. Ideally, you will have informal information flows. Work on your political acumen; this is key, so you knowingly and consciously decide how to act instead of being forced into an action without being able to think it through, or being caught off guard and letting your emotions get the better of you. Opportunities may arise that you can grasp before they are officially announced and or opened to everyone. Threats can be seen before they surface. The trick is to be aware of what is happening, but try not to get involved; this is as hard as it sounds! And, if you do have to get involved, make sure it is to your benefit and not detriment.

- In more political cultures, consider Baddeley & James mode for political awareness and game playing. The above model identifies four animal personas:
  - Game playing/politically unaware = the inept donkey
  - Game playing/politically aware = the clever fox
  - Politically unaware/acts with integrity = innocent sheep
  - Politically aware/acts with integrity = wise owl

When considering the landscape, it can be helpful to use this analysis. Also, don't forget to use it on yourself. Where are you on this model? If you're a sheep, you know what foxes do to sheep!

Game playing/politically unaware is the braying inept donkey, similar to sheep, but is internally focused on themselves.

Politically unaware/but acting with integrity, is the innocent and naïve sheep, loyal and hard working, but directionless by themselves.

Politically aware/acting with integrity is the wise owl who sits above the forest and can see what is directly below and far out into the forest.

Politically aware/game-playing is the cunning and clever fox. The fox can cause damage to all the animals, but its main target is the sheep. They act out of self-interest.

I use this model in coaching, and ask my mentees and coachees where a leader should sit. Most say the owl, one or two have said fox. The answer I was once given was that a leader should mainly sit in the owl box, but with a bit of the fox in them. Otherwise, the owl can be played – or worse, become the fox's victim. This is where the True Leader stands apart: they recognise their own False God tendencies, know how to work alongside False Gods, and understand how to manage them.

Chapter Six

Leadership & Culture

"The only thing of real importance that leaders do is to create and manage culture."
– Edgar Schein

I was very fortunate, as early in my career, I had the opportunity to work for some organisations which had strong cultures. People were happy, there was great teamwork, we worked hard and the organisations had great results. It wasn't utopia, but as organisational cultures go, they were good. Later on in my career, I wasn't so fortunate. Some organisations were the opposite – bad and operationally weak. I noticed that people were not happy. They were frustrated, there was friction or, in some cases, bullying, and the results were not good. In fact, not only were the results not good, but the organisations were also exposed to tribunals, legal claims and more.

Obviously, I preferred being happy in my role, working in great teams that got along and knew how to settle differences. And, like most, I didn't like working in the bad cultures for all the reasons above. From an organisational perspective, it usually translates into poor results, which equals no bonuses and the possibility of redundancies.

This became a bigger problem for me when I went into change and transformation, as it literally was my job to help people navigate change. It was hard to do in a good and strong culture, but much harder in a bad and weak culture. This started my journey of becoming a Cultural Anthropologist. Now, I study and work with organisations that want to change their culture or aspects of their organisation that will impact it. It became more than just doing my job well. I am passionate about creating environments that enable all people to thrive, do good, be good and make money. Who doesn't want that?

I have spent the last few years examining the link between a strong and good culture and optimal financial performance. Li et al conducted a study titled "Dissecting Corporate Culture Using Generative AI – Insights from Analyst Reports." This fascinating research, made possible by AI, analysed over 2.4 million reports referencing organisational culture and its connection to business performance – both financial and non-financial.[1] The key relational values identified were innovation, adaptability and customer focus. Organisations exhibiting these values saw greater growth, improved profits and more satisfied employees. The main drivers were the leadership team, the arrival of new leadership following mergers and acquisitions and the organisation's strategy. While the link between strong culture and financial performance is well-established, this data reinforces prior research and validates earlier findings.

There are many drivers which lead an organisation to have a good and strong culture, and one of the biggest drivers is the leader(s).

Edgar Schein, a renowned business theorist and organisational psychologist, argues that a leader's primary role is to shape and guide organisational culture. But can culture truly be created and managed? Many academics – such as Schein, McGregor, Burns and Bass, Cameron and Quinn, Kotter and Heskett, and Johnson and Scholes – believe it can. If not, the risks are considerable, as seen in the high-profile failures of PurpleCo, RBS and Yahoo. On a smaller scale, an unmanaged culture can lead to everyday issues: unhappy and unproductive staff, rising sickness, high attrition, poor service and more.

As we have spent a considerable amount of time exploring the unhappy path of emerging leadership, I was mindful that it would be beneficial to remind ourselves of what a happy path looks like, through the lens of culture, the role of leaders and the power it has to make or break leaders.

Satya Nadella was born in 1967 in India. Educated in both India (an Engineering degree) and the US (Master's in Computer Science and an MBA), he joined Microsoft in 1992. He got a reputation for being a good leader, as he was both technically brilliant and collaborative, and contributed in several areas. He was appointed Chief Executive Officer (CEO) in 2014 and took over at a time when Microsoft was struggling. It had a reputation for being cutthroat, political and stuck in its ways. He relied on "culture shock to drive growth", shifting the culture to prioritise empathy, collaboration, a growth mindset (inspired by Carol Dweck), continuous learning and innovation. He also did it in a sustainable way, as he believes that "organisations should not be measured so much during a CEO's tenure, but after. Because if it all falls apart after you have gone, then you haven't created an organisation that is enduring.[2] This holds up in the analysis of Microsoft's performance within its competitor pool and Glassdoor scores over time.

In the years that followed, Microsoft's market value tripled, it successfully acquired brands such as LinkedIn and GitHub to support growth, and it surpassed Apple as the world's most valuable company. The research says that under his CEO leadership, the stock price went up by over 800%.

He is currently Microsoft's CEO and Chairman, having taken on the latter role in 2021. His leadership has faced criticism, for instance, his "completely wrong" comment suggesting women should trust the system to receive equal pay. He later issued a full public apology. Another controversy involved the launch of Tay.ai, a Twitter bot that was quickly corrupted into a "venom-spewing racist". The project was shut down, and Microsoft again apologised. "In the old days of Microsoft, heads surely would have rolled. But Nadella... sent the Tay. ai team a note of encouragement. 'Keep pushing, and know that I am with you,' he wrote in an email, urging staffers to take the criticism in the right spirit while exercising 'deep empathy' for anyone hurt by Tay. (The) key is to keep learning and improving."[3]

In a nod to the chapter's main quote, Nadella believes "my job is curation of our culture … if you don't focus on creating a culture that allows people to do their best work, then you have created nothing."[4] Following his success, he has received multiple public accolades.

Outside of work, he likes poetry, cricket and continuous learning. He is also father to three children, two daughters and a son, the latter now sadly deceased. His son Zain was born blind, quadriplegic and with cerebral palsy. He passed in February 2022, at 26 years old. Nadella shares his experiences publicly about raising a child with special needs, but also how that has helped him be a better leader. After achieving so much professionally, he "has come with a sense of responsibility, one that focuses on not just the next quarterly report but the legacy he will leave behind." He published a book called *Hit Refresh* in 2017, which covers the "quest to rediscover Microsoft's Soul and imagine a better future for everyone."[5] It was a *New York Times* best seller, and the profits from the book were donated to Microsoft's Philanthropies arm.

Nadella's story is incredibly powerful. By reshaping the culture, he was able to not just help his organisation go from strength to strength, but he also started to build a legacy that was bigger than himself, trying to empower others to do the same personally and professionally.

Oscar Wilde says, "Be yourself; everyone else is already taken." You need to lead in a style that is yours and be "workthentic." Once you have found your style and leadership identity, the next area to focus on is becoming a cultural architect (which hopefully you have been developing, like Nadella did).

The aim of this book was not to publish a blueprint for leadership, as there are too many variables. However, Nadella has many of the hallmarks of a Real Model/True Leader, and should be taken as a great example.

What Do We Mean by "Culture"

Culture is one of those words we all think we understand, yet it's often used so broadly that it loses meaning. I've seen many leaders speak about culture without truly grasping what it entails. I've seen strategies where different departments each push for their own version – a safety culture, a happy and relaxed culture, a cyber-resilient culture, a data-driven culture, a client-centric culture, an employee-first culture, an entrepreneurial culture, a risk-focused culture and so on. It's no surprise there are so many cultural clashes within organisations.

The above section talks to the high-level theme of what we expect culture to be, but organisational culture is really just "what the group has learned in its efforts to survive, grow, deal with its external environment, and organise itself."[6]

The first thing I do is work out how an organisation has organised itself. The next step in understanding the true meaning of the word "culture" and its implications for an organisation is to examine the various elements that comprise it. This is where the use of Hall's Cultural Iceberg is of help.

The social-psychological school of psychology focuses on how people's behaviours are influenced by the actual or imagined influence of others. The Culture Iceberg, developed by Edward Hall, bridges the gap between psychology and anthropology, explaining a culture's observable and unobservable dynamics. It also shows that most of an organisation's culture is below the surface.

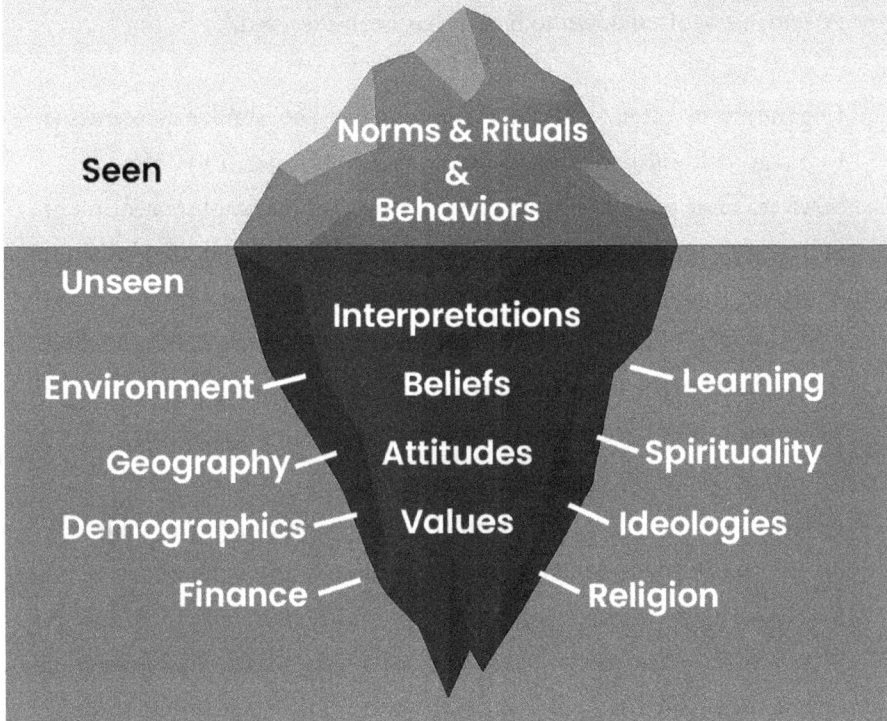

The Cultural Iceberg

Seen

Norms & Rituals & Behaviors

Unseen

Interpretations

Environment — Beliefs — Learning

Geography — Attitudes — Spirituality

Demographics — Values — Ideologies

Finance — — Religion

At the top of the iceberg, above the water, you have elements like behaviours and practices. Lower down, under the water, you have the unobservable elements like norms, rules, attitudes and beliefs.

The iceberg also considers external factors that can impact an organisation's culture, such as economics, media and geography. For example, COVID-19 changed a number of organisational practices, such as hybrid working, social distancing, masks and more. At a macro level, as human beings, we are part of many cultures, some too vast to be fully controlled, but often leaders shape, influence and engage in behavioural nudges to drive a certain action. However, organisational culture is somewhat smaller than large social systems, but those same tactics are sometimes used. The outputs can lead to varying degrees of effectiveness, often down to how it has been executed.[7]

Organisations often conduct surveys, audits and similar assessments to gauge cultural dynamics. Most major consulting firms offer these services. Time and money are spent on surveys that capture sentiment at a single moment – and by the time results are shared, they're often outdated. In one case, a survey was conducted just after upsetting job role announcements – you can imagine the sentiment! In my view, these efforts often skim the surface, which is why so much is missed when trying to understand an organisation's cultural dynamics.

I conducted an analysis based on the outputs of a major consultancy on a strategic cultural alignment. The outputs were gathered based on a wishful, faulty premise, with a narrow and biased participant group. The outputs were then shared with leadership, and they were not questioned, which led the leadership team down the wrong path. It was only down to luck that the research became moot, due to a further strategic change in direction. Had it not been and the recommendations being followed up on, there would have been a very costly fallout.

Leaders as Cultural Shapers, Engineers and Architects

The impact of culture, and whether a leader can influence it, was explored with the Leadership Participant Group. All, bar one, believed that leaders are cultural engineers. But only 28% had done or seen purposeful interventions to shape either a part of the culture or all of it. The other 72% acknowledged a leader had shaped culture, but not intentionally.

My work involves designing cultural change plans and looking at interventions to align strategy and culture. I help leaders get the culture they want. If managed effectively, it can be highly successful, resulting in improved financial and non-financial performance. In one case, it reduced volatility on the balance sheet, achieved optimal financial performance despite headwinds, increased visibility on an award-winning innovation, and improved the organisation's levels of attrition.

Not all leaders can change culture. Participant 9 shared an example of how a toxic culture had infected a good leader, causing them to become bad themselves. It was too big, too ingrained and infected him. This contrasts with Nadella's experience; it didn't infect him, but it wasn't until he was in the CEO seat that he was in a position to start designing and implementing culture change. Emerging leaders will only be able to influence the culture of their area, not the whole enterprise, but a small corner of the world is better than nothing.

Culture change being done to a leader(s) has been documented in Mergers and Acquisitions (M&A) horror stories. One of the worst M&A failures is that of the 1998 Daimler-Benz and Chrysler merger, which cost $37 billion. This is an example of when culture wasn't managed, and how it impacted two famous brands. In this case, the leadership team seemed to stay loyal to their original organisations. As leaders, they did not succeed in shaping a shared culture, and it appeared neither group aligned to even agree on joint decision making, let alone the organisational culture.

The vision was to "create a trans-Atlantic car-making powerhouse," but this never materialised. Cultural clashes were a major factor. Daimler-Benz operated in a formal, hierarchical and data-driven manner, with decisions made through structured processes. In contrast, Chrysler had a more informal, risk-taking culture where decisions were made flexibly. The leadership teams functioned very differently. Although presented as a merger of equals, Daimler-Benz held operational control, something that did not sit well with Chrysler's employees, resulting in the loss of key staff. Additionally, the legal landscape around employee management differed significantly between Germany and the US. These conflicts meant the merger's vision went unrealised.[8] In 2007, Chrysler was sold for USD 7 billion to a management firm. Their difficulties continued, culminating in bankruptcy and, eventually, a rescue and sale to Fiat in 2009.

In some cases, merging two leadership teams and cultures can be beneficial, provided meaningful cultural work is carried out. As noted in the study by Li et al, Participant 9 described working in a toxic culture that improved following an acquisition. A stricter HR team was introduced, and "the place got better."[9] Whether cultural change is driven internally or externally, it must be actively addressed, even if the conclusion is that no action is required. Expertise is essential; when mishandled or when the wrong tools are used, the outcome can be nearly as damaging as doing nothing. One crucial focus area – often hidden beneath the surface – is the organisation's cultural norms.

Cultural and Societal Norms Through the Lens of "Playing the Game"

Organisations' cultures will have their own norms, rules, etc. Some are written, some are not. It takes place behind the scenes, with a shadow side and unwritten rules. These "tangible and intangible aspects that must be understood.[10]

Behavioural socialisation is the process through which individuals learn to conform to societal norms – an instinct rooted in the need for survival. When there's a conflict between personal values and those of a workplace culture, the result can be emotional strain or, in some cases, organisational failure, as seen with Daimler-Benz and Chrysler in 1998. AnthrOrg's Cultural Assessment Model (ACAM)® measures this tension, recognising how widespread value conflict can severely impact a culture. For example, if the average person processes around 4 to 7 thoughts at once, and some of that mental bandwidth is consumed by navigating toxic norms or value clashes, productivity will inevitably drop. At worst, internal and external conflicts emerge, countercultures form, and projects derail. When multiple projects fail, strategic objectives collapse, ultimately reflecting a failure of leadership.

Often, when people speak to a person who "[knows] how to play the game," it is because they know the unwritten rules or norms of the organisation, and how to play them well. Sometimes these rules are well-known and entrenched, sometimes they are the opposite. A good example would be looking at a leadership team made up of the same gender, ethnicity, and socioeconomic background, claiming to be inclusive and supportive of female leadership, but there are no females in the leadership team. As they are in charge of encouraging and discouraging female leaders joining, and looking at their behaviour, it suggests females are not part of their team; it is unlikely a woman would succeed in getting to that team.

The norm is that women aren't really invited to play the game. The job of a cultural change expert would be to understand the dynamics, or the unwritten rules, and then implement interventions to rewrite them. Almost like organisational neuroplasticity.

It is not the sole responsibility of a leader to shape culture. Oversight is the responsibility of an organisation's Board.

The role of the Board in governing, especially bad behaviour, is key. Padilla et al found that "strong oversight by a board of directors is necessary."[11] For boards to govern effectively, certain conditions are essential. They include board independence, with a critical mass of outside members not hand-picked by the CEO; policy-level oversight by the board in company affairs, including performance reviews and succession processes; and board accountability, where the board is responsible for executive and organisational performance and has the power to sanction executives.

Aligning Strategy and Culture

Peter Drucker is often referred to as the father of modern management, and one of his well-known and perhaps overused quotes is, "Culture eats strategy for breakfast." Part of a leader's role is to devise and implement a strategy, usually to hit financial targets. Therefore, considering what is at stake, why are leaders not doing more to intentionally shape their organisation's culture? What are the boards doing to make sure this is being done? And, more importantly, do they know what dynamics, norms, games and rules are really affecting their organisation's cultural dynamics and a leader's ability to succeed?

The previously mentioned 28%/72% split reflects how the Participant Leadership group viewed intentional versus unintentional cultural leadership. Only 28% believed leaders had actively invested in strategic culture change; the remainder saw culture evolve by accident. The outcomes in the latter group illustrate the risks of leaving culture to chance.

Interestingly, this aligns with a well-known statistic: 70% of change initiatives fail – a figure often attributed to research by McKinsey. The root causes of these failures are frequently cultural. Applying the logic loosely, could the high failure rate be linked to leaders who failed to manage culture deliberately, instead leaving success to chance?

While we lack comprehensive data to draw a direct correlation, the work by Li et al offers a meaningful bridge. It would be insightful to examine whether the organisations that the Participant Leadership group identified as investing in intentional culture work were outperforming their competitors, possibly because they were better equipped to implement change and execute strategy. The data analysed by Li et al reinforces earlier research showing that culture has a positive impact on both financial and non-financial performance.[12] So, the question remains: Why do nearly 70% of leaders appear content to be the architects of their own failure?

Leaving It All to Chance?

"Sometimes an organisation's culture may shift in unwanted ways that take time for leaders to recognise, and then it's too late. Rather than trusting your gut about what's going on, conduct a regular culture assessment to gather evidence on the lived experiences of employees across your organisation."[13] But, this does need to go beyond surveys, which never really get past the tip of the socio-cultural iceberg.

For the approximately 70% of leaders leaving culture to chance, you seem to be taking an unnecessary risk. Those who don't leave it to chance do the work needed to involve professionals, as poor work can be just as dangerous as leaving it all to chance. From a more negative perspective, consider what games, norms, and other behaviours might already be working against a leader's success.

Emerging leaders, you haven't gone through the trials and tribulations of stepping into leadership just to have culture trip you up. Manage and monitor it.

Summary

This chapter explores the critical relationship between leadership and organisational culture, emphasising the role of leaders as cultural architects. Edgar Schein's assertion that the most important thing leaders do is to create and manage culture serves as a foundation for understanding the immense responsibility leaders bear in shaping organisational environments. By highlighting various real-world examples, including the toxic leadership cultures and successful cultural transformations within organisations, this chapter demonstrates how culture is not just a passive reflection of leadership; it is a dynamic force that leaders actively craft and influence. When a False God is at the helm of an organisation, it can suffer; a Real Model or True Leader aims to create a good culture, which can lead to superior financial performance. That being said, there are many layers and nuances to this, and as seen in chapter 4, some False Gods can be successful at least from a short-term perspective, as illustrated by the case study of Hank shared by Participant 14 (Sushi).

The golden thread throughout this discussion is the undeniable impact that culture has on leadership effectiveness and organisational success. Whether a False God, Real Model or True Leader, the culture they nurture will shape their ability to lead, their decision-making, and the overall success of their organisation. The examples of failed mergers and toxic work environments contrast sharply with the successes of organisations that have intentionally cultivated positive cultures. These examples make it clear that cultural management is not just a peripheral concern. Rather, it is central to a company's survival and growth.

Culture is the heartbeat of any organisation. It shapes the way people work, interact, and perform. In today's rapidly changing and volatile business environment (the VUCA landscape), organisations cannot afford to ignore their culture. Leaders must understand that their influence over culture is profound, and failing to manage it means leaving the organisation vulnerable to dysfunction, disengagement, toxicity, and failure. The statistics on failed change projects, for instance, suggest that much of this failure is rooted in neglecting cultural dynamics, highlighting that culture is a powerful determinant of success or failure. From a personal perspective, it could mean the difference between being employable or not.

Leaders must recognise the importance of being cultural shapers, engineers and architects. It is not enough to leave culture to chance. Purposeful, intentional interventions are required to shape the values, behaviours, and norms that drive organisational performance. This involves regularly assessing the culture, taking action to address any toxic elements and ensuring that the culture is aligned with the organisation's strategic goals.

If nothing is done, the risks can be substantial. The failure to actively shape culture is not a neutral act. As highlighted, inaction on culture can lead to organisational decline, much like the examples of Daimler-Benz and Chrysler, where cultural misalignment led to a multi-billion-dollar failure. But management of culture must be multidimensional and not solely based on engagement surveys, which will give a delayed feedback loop of superficial sentiment.

Leadership and culture are inextricably linked. Leaders must take responsibility for shaping culture, understanding its power, and actively intervening to guide it in a positive direction. Doing so is not just beneficial but essential for long-term success in an increasingly complex and challenging business environment.

Reflections and Actions

- Don't assume you know what culture is and how it works. Develop your Cultural Quotient (CQ) and start building your awareness of how language, rituals, decision-making and informal norms shape team culture.

- Start acting as a cultural architect, intentionally modelling and reinforcing the behaviours, language and values you want to see in your area. Could you be the next Nadella?

- Embed culture into strategic execution and ensure that your business decisions, structures and incentives reinforce the desired culture, not undermine it.

- Do you know "how to play the game" and the unofficial rules of your organisation? I have built some information on this called the Culture Compass, which can be found online in the resources hub. Make sure your personal board has a cultural gatekeeper, and ensure you have informal information flows. Also, use situation awareness to make sure you know if the rules of the game shift.

- Be vigilant for toxic patterns and people. Regularly assess and root out dysfunctions, even if performance looks good on the surface; short-term wins can mask long-term damage.

- Observe and learn from cultures around you. Look at what feels energising versus toxic in the team you're part of and consider what leadership behaviours contribute to those dynamics.

- Manage and monitor your own bit of the world. You will ultimately be judged on whether you are delivering against strategy; don't let culture be the thing that trips you up.

Chapter Seven

Conclusion & the Anatomy of a True Leader

"For a True Leader, leadership isn't just a job.
It is simply who they are."
– Heather Connery

Leadership is an ancient construct. The primary reason humanity has progressed from tribal fire circles to global systems is due to effective leadership. From those who first gathered others around fires, to those who built cities and industries, challenged injustice, crossed oceans and explored the stars – humanity's progress has always been driven by leadership. Indeed, there are no known human societies without some form of leadership.[1-3] The story of humanity is, in many ways, the story of leadership.

And yet, for all the bruises and battles (real and metaphorical), leadership is also one of the most meaningful callings there is. At its best, it enables humans to build something greater than ourselves, making things better for others. A True Leader doesn't just manage tasks; they shape culture, spark possibility, protect what matters and make others feel seen, safe, and capable. That's no small thing, especially considering the positive impact it has had on its followers.

Participant 36 explored what it meant for leadership to be part of a person's character or whether it is just a job. The book often links the two concepts interchangeably in the main chapters. For a True Leader, there is no distinction; it simply is who they are, and often they will gravitate toward leadership, even if they weren't born to it.

Whilst it is hard and challenging, there is joy in seeing someone mentored and thriving. There is meaning in navigating tough times with grace, where possible. There is deep personal growth in discovering, as a leader, your voice and values, and in choosing integrity over ego, again and again. Leading is deeply rewarding.

In 2023, the global economy was estimated to be worth $110 trillion. Most professional fields – medicine, academia, accountancy, etc – require rigorous training and qualifications. Yet, despite the enormous influence leaders have over such vast economic value, leadership remains one of the few roles where an unqualified "False God" can step in without formal credentials. There is no mandatory qualification for leadership, and much of the traditional leadership development literature feels more like fantasy than reality. Unlike other professions, a leader can assume immense power without meaningful training, ethical evaluation or accountability to any defined benchmark.

The above is why False Gods can still walk into leadership roles unchecked. They can operate without insight, accountability or consequence. Often, checks and balances are so bureaucratic and take time that the damage has already been done before the data has been analysed. Whilst some of these False Gods pay the price, do they really for each life and resource that is ruined, drained or damaged? In today's VUCA world, it does more than present a risk; it is an inevitability.

Humanity is facing a leadership crisis. As False Gods chase control and image, many Real Models are burning out or opting out whilst trying to navigate today's VUCA landscape. An article in *Forbes* highlighted a "dramatic rise" in CEOs resigning, pointing to burnout, unrelenting pressures, and a lack of readiness to adapt to rapid change.[4] Much of the traditional leadership canon that remains is too Disneyfied, too shallow, too detached from the reality of what it really means to lead. A significant gap in the global leadership pipeline is emerging. Will these lead to more False Gods with their own brand of faux leadership slipping into leadership positions?

Checks and controls are part of governance; this book shows the information on yet another powerful aspect of governance, followship. Followers also need to take accountability for the power they have, and not just look at the LinkedIn version of a Leader. When evaluating the reality of a leader, it is not to find fault in innocuous missteps, but to ask what is happening underneath the surface. If an Emperor has no clothes on, don't follow them for fashion advice on their new Spring/ Summer collection.

Where leadership exists, power also exists – and power always comes with risk. It can lift people or tear them down. It can serve the many, or it can serve only the self. History shows us this time and time again. For every leader who moved a generation forward, there was one who dragged it backwards. This is why leadership is not neutral; it is a moral responsibility. It must be earned, nurtured, checked and re-checked. False Gods often jump into the fire, believing they won't get burned, or worse, end up as barbecued lamb. Some people mistakenly believe that cruelty is a sign of strength or view their team's suffering as a character-building experience. But Real Models often know first-hand that fire burns. They understand pain. And they learn something vital: Don't walk into the flames.

Sometimes, leadership is knowing when not to act. Not every fight is that of the current leader. Not every cliff deserves to be leapt from, especially if it's made of glass, or there is a not-so-trusted supervisor standing right behind with a jealous look in their eye. One of the hardest things for a doer/fixer/problem solver is having the courage to do nothing other than to walk away, to protect internal peace or to decline an ill-fitting opportunity. This may be one of the most under-appreciated acts of leadership and often invites criticism.

Leadership is not all bad, but neither is it the glossy LinkedIn version. It is not a carefully curated highlight reel. It is messy, human, imperfect, political, emotional and exhausting – but it can also be uplifting, powerful and purposeful.

This book was never meant to provide a blueprint for leadership, but is a principle-based reflection. Because there is no one-size-fits-all model. There are traits, tools, frameworks, and theories, but ultimately, True Leadership is an internal and contextual journey. It is shaped by culture, character, capability and circumstance.

And so, this book proposes two new archetypes.

The first is the Real Model. An imperfect but principled leader who tries, reflects and seeks to do the right thing – though not always perfectly. They value people and process. They hold the line and carry the cost. They care, learn and grow. They bruise, but keep going. They are the backbone of most functioning organisations.

The second archetype is the True Leader. This is the leader who goes beyond the Real Model. They don't just survive; they evolve. They, like the Real Model, are not flawless. They lift others and leave behind something stronger than when they arrived. They transcend titles and accolades. This archetype is guided by principles and manifested through action. People are complex and situations are nuanced; every True Leader will have a bit of False God in them, it is for them to check this (and organisations to have the right checks and balances in place).

The False God is not counted. As it is a leader in name or title only, it is often driven by ego, control or performance at any cost. They are capable of having a profound short-term impact, but often leave behind confusion, fear or destruction. When the mask slips, it reveals something damaging. Culture under their reign becomes brittle or toxic. This is not really a new archetype, just a collective title for a bad, faux or incompetent leader.

True Leaders do not have to be born with the leadership gene; they develop the character and skills and grow through experience, adapting to changing environments and learning from failure. The journey from manager to leader is deeply personal and requires a profound shift in identity, often multiple times.

The Anatomy of a True Leader

- **Strong Emotional Intelligence (EI)** - EI shows up in a True Leader as appreciation of others' humanity. Most people are good and want to do a good job; they know when to exercise diplomacy and when a firmer hand is needed. They make others feel safe and seen, they communicate with clarity and workthenticity®. This capability can be rooted in a False God, a Real Model, or a True Leader, but how it is used and the intent behind it determine a True Leader.

- **Technical Proficiency** - This shows up when a leader invests in time to build on competencies and specialities. It also shows up when a leader recognises that a great team is made up of many experts and that one leader is not expected to be the expert in everything. This capability is rooted in the Real Model and True Leader.

- **Effective Decision Maker** - A True Leader will use data to help make decisions, but also look beyond the data. They listen to their gut but also apply good judgment. They rely on principles and values to help guide. They accept the risks and look for the opportunities in wicked decisions. They have the courage and compassion to make tough decisions. This capability is rooted in the Real Model and True Leader.

- **Respected** - They inspire respect by having clarity of self and values, and are real and grounded. They respect themselves and others and earn trust through consistency and fairness. A False God will elicit it to start, and to a specific type of follower, they may even maintain it despite evidence suggesting otherwise, driving an almost cult mentality. From a sustainability perspective, it is the Real Model and True Leader who is truly respected.

- **Collaborative** - They seek input to help make better decisions and deliver projects more effectively. They work to foster an environment where people feel valued and heard. They don't just think internally, but externally, thinking of trade partners or even competitors for industry challenges. They are always mindful of the ultimate client or beneficiary. A False God will elicit it to start, at least superficially, but often only to gather intel. From a sustainability perspective, it is the Real Model and True Leader who embodies this trait.

- **Visionary** - They will look to the future, understand current dynamics and not forget the past. They will devise a strategy and plan to meet the demands and opportunities for tomorrow successfully, bringing their team(s) with them. They maintain relevance and evolve with the times. This is the mark of a True Leader. If raised by a False God, it will either be parroting another's ideas or creating an "us versus them" approach.

- **Inspirational** - They are inspirational both in their work ethic and efforts. They work harder and smarter, and do not overwork. They lead by example and produce positive outcomes. This is rooted in a Real Model and True Leader.

- **Innovative** - Inspire and encourage creativity to help deliver new products and services by sparking possibilities and ideas in others. They are prepared to fail fast but will then likely succeed sooner. The False God, barring some notable outliers, will generally harness the intellectual property of others as their own. Often, more attributable to Real Models and True Leaders.

- **Puts the Grit in Integrity** - Sometimes, it's easier to take the easy way out, but nothing worth fighting for is ever easy. That being said, they also know when to step back or walk away. When they make a mistake, they own it, take responsibility and earn back the dressing room. They work to build trust with others. They check the element of the False God within. They make time to be a True Leader even when they don't have time (Participant 16).

- **Leads From the Front** - They know when and how to effectively take a stand, without killing themselves (metaphorically) to do it. They do the right thing, even when no one is looking. They exhibit determination and resolve (Participant 37). This is rooted in Real Models and True Leaders.

- **Wise** - They embrace the power to learn and unlearn. They aim to be the best leaders they can be and forgive themselves when they have made a mistake. They listen to doubt and use it as a self-audit (Participant 36). They maintain situational awareness and understand power dynamics. They seek to find the peace within, whilst weathering a storm. This is rooted in a True Leader.

- **Cultural Architect** - They shape today and tomorrow's social systems, strategies and culture. They seek to develop a good or high Cultural Quotient (CQ). They create a good and strong culture, one that's sustainable and enables others to thrive. They lift others and leave behind something stronger than when they arrived. This is rooted in a True Leader.

The book also challenges overused terms like "authenticity," replacing them with more useful and practical approaches like "workthenticity," which is the ability to bring your best, most appropriate self to work, rather than some idealised or "unedited" version. It explores the tension between being who and what is needed. People have various aspects to their personality. Take Bob, for example. Bob could be a nurturing father, loving husband, respectful grandson, dedicated footballer and someone who parties hard on the weekend while being a diplomatic Managing Director. All these facets bleed into one another, but party hard Bob would not show up for Sunday dinner with his grandmother. Bob's Managing Director facets, benefits from all of his, but he brings out the most appropriate of those to work. Unhelpful guidance around being your authentic self at work is as unhelpful as "women can have it all," where a whole generation ran themselves ragged trying to do!

One area that had its own chapter was the importance of culture, leading to an understanding of how it shapes a leader, as well as how a leader can shape their culture. Culture is the heartbeat of any organisation, influencing behaviours, decision-making and overall performance.

Leaders play a pivotal role in shaping and sustaining culture by modelling desired behaviours, reinforcing values and creating environments that promote psychological safety and inclusivity. Leaders acting as cultural architects who shape and influence the environments they govern. The success or failure of an organisation often hinges not just on the decisions made by its leaders and the successful execution of its strategy, but also on the organisational culture it fosters, which can either enable or hinder success. Leaders must not only navigate their own leadership challenges but also manage the dynamic forces of culture, which can either support or undermine their strategic objectives. A strong, positive culture enhances engagement, innovation and resilience, as well as optimal performance, which can create successful finance performance and outperform competitors. And it unpacks culture not as a soft sidenote, but as critical to a leader's success. Culture shapes leadership, and leaders shape culture. Leaders act as cultural architects, whether consciously or unconsciously. And when culture is ignored, the cost is vast.

This book is a companion for those who are entering emerging leadership, already in it or aspiring to become an emerging leader. It also encourages followers to consider their level of accountability and provokes organisations to think about what is needed for them to nurture True Leaders. They must empower Real Models to become True Leaders, and help Real Models when they do have False God traits. That means trusting people with power and letting them fail – with the appropriate guardrails. That means not punishing the first misstep. It means recognising that wisdom is not taught in workshops but cultivated through safe, supported experience. A lot is said about being given the trust, space and time to learn, but also to make mistakes. By giving team members autonomy and a say in decision-making, leaders instil a sense of ownership and responsibility. This empowerment not only boosts confidence but also allows emerging leaders to develop critical thinking and problem-solving skills, says Dr Lyn Corbett. "They will make mistakes. That's part of the process. It's important to provide a safe environment for leaders to learn from their mistakes so they can make more informed decisions in the future."[5]

Leadership development must become real. Less theory, more truth. Less Disney, more grit. Training must account for the lived mess of modern leadership: wicked decision-making, corporate bruises, navigating the politics of influence and the pain of letting people down. And yes, power needs to be part of the curriculum. I hope this book contributes to the leadership development canon, a manual of what not to do. By capturing this, I hope to give the reader an unfair advantage, allowing them to avoid some of the challenges leadership presents.

To say leadership is a journey is reductive but true. Whilst there is a lot to it, there are also realities such as the average time to reach the C-Suite. This leaves plenty of time to help emerging leaders develop their leadership skills in practice as they progress through succession plans.

As the world digitises, automates and accelerates, the human side of leadership becomes more important, not less. AI will help, but it cannot replace the complexity, ethics, empathy and lived wisdom of True Leadership. That being said, the two can complement each other.

There is no perfect leader. But there are those who lead with courage, wisdom, humility and peace – even amid the storm. They still choose to lead despite the challenges, which is when it matters most. That is the anatomy of a True Leader. And the world needs more of you now than ever.

The work of becoming a True Leader doesn't stop with the last page. If the ideas in this book resonated with you, I'd love to continue the dialogue. You'll find more about my work and ways to connect on the *About the Author* page. But above all, I hope you carry these lessons forward into the way you lead every day.

References

Introduction

1. Pfeffer, J., *Leadership BS: Fixing Workplaces and Careers One Truth at a Time* (New York: Harper Business, 2015).

2. Van Vugt, M., 'The Evolutionary Origins of Leadership and Followership', *Personality and Social Psychology Review*, 10 (2006), pp. 354–371.

3. Kharpal, A., 'Amazon CEO Jeff Bezos Has a Pretty Good Idea of Quarterly Earnings 3 Years in Advance', *CNBC* (8 May 2017), available at: https://www.cnbc.com/2017/05/08/amazon-ceo-jeff-bezos-long-term-thinking.html [accessed 14 April 2025].

4. Johansen, B. *Leaders Make the Future: Ten New Leadership Skills for an Uncertain World.* Berrett-Koehler, (2012).

5. Leonhard, G., 'Digital Transformation: Are You Ready for Exponential Change?' (2016), available at: https://www.youtube.com/watch?v=ystdF6jN7hc [accessed 14 April 2025].

6. Rittel, H.W.J. and Webber, M.M., 'Dilemmas in a General Theory of Planning', *Policy Sciences*, 4 (1973), pp. 155–169.

7. Spencer Stuart, *UK Insurance CEO Route to the Top* (2018), available at: https://www.spencerstuart.com/research-and-insight/uk-insurance-ceo-route-to-the-top [accessed 14 April 2025].

8. Spencer Stuart, *UK Spencer Stuart Board Index* (2024), available at: https://www.spencerstuart.com/research-and-insight/uk-board-index/the-board [accessed 14 April 2025].

Chapter 1

1. Wikipedia, 'The Art of War', *Wikipedia: The Free Encyclopedia*, last modified June 2025, available at: https://en.wikipedia.org/wiki/The_Art_of_War [accessed 5 August 2025].

2. Krause, D.G., *The Art of War for Executives*, 2nd edn (London: Nicholas Brealey Publishing, 2002).

3. Ibid.

4. Machiavelli, N., *The Prince*, trans. by Bondanella, P. and Virgil, M. (Oxford: Oxford University Press, 2008).

5. Schein, E.H. and Schein, P.A., *Organisational Culture and Leadership*, 5th edn (Hoboken, NJ: Wiley, 2017).

6. Weston, S., *Leadership*, 3rd edn (London: Sage, 2019).

7. Ibid.

8. Schedlitzki, D. and Edwards, G., *Studying Leadership,* 2nd edn (London: Sage, 2018).

9. Kets de Vries, M.F.R., *Leaders, Fools and Impostors: Essays on the Psychology of Leadership* (iUniverse, 2003).

10. Boddy, C.R., Miles, D., Sanyal, C. and Hartog, M., 'Leadership, Corporate Strategy and Financial Performance', *International Journal of Business and Management,* 5.12 (2010), pp. 1–14.

11. Schedlitzki and Edwards, *Studying Leadership.*

12. Hemphill, J.K., *Leaders and Their Followers* (New York: Free Press, 1961).

13. Stogdill, R.M., *Handbook of Leadership: A Survey of Theory and Research* (New York: Free Press, 1974).

14. Hollander, E.P., *Leadership and Power* (New York: Free Press, 1985).

15. Brown, M.E., *Organisational Culture* (London: Pitman, 1991).

16. Bass, B.M., *Bass & Stogdill's Handbook of Leadership: Theory, Research, and Managerial Applications,* 3rd edn (New York: Free Press, 1990).

17. Van Vugt, 'The Evolutionary Origins of Leadership and Followership'.

18. Padilla, A., Hogan, R. and Kaiser, R.B., 'The Toxic Triangle: Destructive Leaders, Susceptible Followers, and Conducive Environments', *The Leadership Quarterly*, 18 (2007), pp. 176–194.

19. Smith, J., *Good Self, Bad Self: How to Bounce Back from a Personal Crisis* (New York: Free Press, 2012).

Chapter 2

1. Arvey, R.D., Rotundo, M., Johnson, W., Zhang, Z. and McGue, M., 'The Genetic Influence on Leadership Role Occupancy', *The Leadership Quarterly*, 17.1 (2006), pp. 1–20.

2. De Neve, J.E., Mikhaylov, S., Dawes, C.T., Christakis, N.A. and Fowler, J.H., 'Born to Lead? A Twin Design and Genetic Association Study of Leadership Role Occupancy', *The Leadership Quarterly*, 24.1 (2013), pp. 45–60.

3. Komives, S.R., Longerbeam, S.D., Owen, J.E., Mainella, F.C. and Osteen, L., 'A Leadership Identity Development Model: Applications from a Grounded Theory', *Journal of College Student Development*, 47.4 (2006), pp. 401–418.

4. Murray, S., 'More Executive MBA Students Look to Switch Careers', *Financial Times* (2024), available at: https://www.ft.com/content/403b1118-6dd8-4d8d-bd2c-a0923fc50c97 [accessed 14 April 2025].

5. Korn Ferry, *Talent Trends 2025: Progress Over Perfection* (2025), available at: https://www.kornferry.com/content/dam/

kornferry-v2/featured-topics/pdf/2025-TA-Trends-Report.pdf [accessed 15 April 2025].

6. Wapnick, E. (2015) "Why some of us don't have one true calling", *TEDx*. Available at https://www.ted.com/talks/emilie_wapnick_why_some_of_us_don_t_have_one_true_calling?referrer=playlist-how_passion_becomes_purpose [accessed 7 April 2025].

7. Arruda, W., 'How to Show You Are a Leader at Work', *Forbes* (2023), available at: https://www.forbes.com/sites/williamarruda/2023/10/10/how-to-show-you-are-a-leader-at-work/?sh=2a0b9ff6161f [accessed 29 February 2024].

8. Forbes, Ettore, M., 'Why Most New Executives Fail – and Four Things Companies Can Do About It', *Forbes* (2020), available at: https://www.forbes.com/councils/forbescoachescouncil/2020/03/13/why-most-new-executives-fail-and-four-things-companies-can-do-about-it/ [accessed 15 April 2025].

9. Ibid.

10. Arruda, 'How to Show You Are a Leader at Work'.

11. Collins, J., *Good to Great: Why Some Companies Make the Leap and Others Don't* (London: Random House, 2001).

12. Schedlitzki, D. and Edwards, G., *Studying Leadership*, 2nd edn (London: Sage, 2018).

13. Ruscio, J. & Amabile, T. M. (1996) "How Does Creativity Happen", *Harvard Business School*.

14. Schedlitzki and Edwards, *Studying Leadership*.

15. Sutton, 'AWEsome Work', *The British Psychological Society* (2020), available at: https://www.bps.org.uk/psychologist/awesome-work [accessed 22 April 2025].

Chapter 3

1. Komives, S.R., Owen, J.E., Longerbeam, S.D., Mainella, F.C. and Osteen, L., 'A Leadership Identity Development Model: Applications from a Grounded Theory', *Journal of College Student Development*, 47.4 (2006), pp. 401–418.

2. Blake, R.R., & Mouton, J.S. (1964). *The Managerial Grid: The Key to Leadership Excellence. Houston, Gulf Publishing Company*.

3. Krause, D.G., *The Art of War for Executives*, 2nd edn (London: Nicholas Brealey Publishing, 2002).

4. Schedlitzki, D. and Edwards, G., *Studying Leadership*, 2nd edn (London: Sage, 2018).

5. Goleman, D., 'What Makes a Leader', *Harvard Business Review* (2004), available at: https://hbr.org/2004/01/what-makes-a-leader [accessed 28 February 2025].

6. Valasquez, L. "Are You Being Emotionally Manipulated at Work?", *Harvard Business Review*, 2024. Available online https://hbr.org/2024/02/are-you-being-emotionally-manipulated-at-work, [accessed at 23 April 2025].

7. Ressa, M., "Time Women of the Year: Amal Clooney Won't Back Down", *Time*, 2022. Available online https://time.com/collection/women-of-the-year/6150539/amal-clooney/ [accessed at 29 February 2024].

8. Rizvi, J., 'Transformative Leadership: The Art of Inspiring Leaders Around You', *Forbes* (2024), available at: https://www.forbes.com/sites/jiawertz/2024/01/20/transformative-leadership-the-art-of-inspiring-leaders-around-you/amp/ [accessed 28 February 2024].

9. Van Vugt, M. and Ahuja, A., *Selected* (London: Profile Books, 2010).

10. Ibid.

11. Masterson, V., '2024 Is a Record Year for Elections. Here's What You Need to Know', *World Economic Forum* (2023), available at: https://www.weforum.org/stories/2023/12/2024-elections-around-world/ [accessed 7 May 2025].

12. Raval, A., 'Competent Jerks — High Performers Who Are Horrible to Colleagues — Have a Shelf Life at the Office', *Financial Post* (29 February 2024), available at: https://financialpost.com/financial-times/competent-jerks-shelf-life-office [accessed 5 August 2025].

13. Van Vugt and Ahuja, *Selected.*

14. Smith, J., *Good Self, Bad Self* (New York: Free Press, 2013).

15. Raval, 'Competent Jerks — High Performers Who Are Horrible to Colleagues'.

16. Valasquez, L., "Are You Being Emotionally Manipulated at Work?", *Harvard Business Review*, 2024. Available online https://hbr.org/2024/02/are-you-being-emotionally-manipulated-at-work [accessed at 23 April 2025].

Chapter 4

1. Komives, S.R., Owen, J.E., Longerbeam, S.D., Mainella, F.C. and Osteen, L., 'A Leadership Identity Development Model: Applications from a Grounded Theory', *Journal of College Student Development*, 47.4 (2006), pp. 401–418.

2. Ibarra, H., *Act Like a Leader, Think Like a Leader* (Boston, MA: Harvard Business Review Press, 2015).

3. Komives et al, "A Leadership Identity Development Model: Applications from a Grounded Theory," *Journal of College Student Development*, 2006.

4. Ibid.

5. DeRue, D.S. and Ashford, S.J., 'Who Will Lead and Who Will Follow? A Social Process of Leadership Identity Construction in Organisations', *Academy of Management Review*, 35.4 (2010), pp. 627–647.

6. Danyal, A. (2024) 'The fine line between confidence and arrogance', *Leadership Right*. Available at: https://www.leadershipright.com/p/the-fine-line-between-confidence-and-arrogance [accessed: 29 February 2024].

7. Bazerman, M.H. and Moore, D.A., *Judgment in Managerial Decision Making*, 8th edn (Hoboken, NJ: Wiley Custom, 2017), chs. 2, 8 and 12.

8. Smith, J., *Good Self, Bad Self: How to Bounce Back from a Personal Crisis* (New York: Free Press, 2012).

9. Collins, J., *Good to Great: Why Some Companies Make the Leap and Others Don't* (New York: Harper Business, 2001).

10. Raval, A., 'Competent Jerks — High Performers Who Are Horrible to Colleagues — Have a Shelf Life at the Office', *Financial Post* (29 February 2024), available at: https://financialpost.com/financial-times/competent-jerks-shelf-life-office [accessed 05 August 2025].

11. Cherry, K., 'Characteristics of Ego Strength', *Verywell Mind* (8 May 2023), available at: https://www.verywellmind.com/ego-strength-2795169 [accessed 05 August 2025].

12. Smith, J., *Good Self, Bad Self*, Free Press, 2012.

Chapter 5

1. Peter, Laurence J., and Raymond Hull, *The Peter Principle: Why Things Always Go Wrong*. Pan Books, [1969] 1970.

2. Wright-Whitlay, A., 'CEOs Tend to Overstay Their Welcome, Hurting Firm Performance, New Study Finds', *Fox School of Business* (2014), available at: https://www.fox.temple.edu/news/ceos-tend-overstay-their-welcome-hurting-firm-performance-new-study-finds [accessed 30 April 2025].

3. Dorsey, K.D., 'From Glass Ceilings to Glass Cliffs: A Guide to Jumping, Not Falling', *MIT Sloan Management Review* (2023), available at: https://sloanreview.mit.edu/article/from-glass-ceilings-to-glass-cliffs-a-guide-to-jumping-not-falling/ [accessed 30 April 2025].

4. Ibid.

5. Krause, D.G., *The Art of War Executives*, 2nd edn (London: Nicholas Brealey Publishing, 2002).

6. Hewlett, S.A. and Buck Luce, C., 'Extreme Jobs: The Dangerous Allure of the 70-Hour Workweek', *Harvard Business Review* (2006), available at: https://hbr.org/2006/12/extreme-jobs-the-dangerous-allure-of-the-70-hour-workweek [accessed 30 April 2025].

7. *Cambridge Dictionary*, s.v. "politics," https://dictionary.cambridge.org/dictionary/english/politics [accessed 24 October 2025].

8. Richards, L., 'Office Politics: How to Handle It', *Intelligent People* (2024), available at: https://www.intelligentpeople.co.uk/employer-advice/office-politics/ [accessed 1 May 2025].

9. Gentle, S., 'A Third of Brits Unhappy at Work Because of Office Politics', *Onrec* (2015), available at: https://www.onrec.com/news/statistics-and-trends/a-third-of-brits-unhappy-at-work-because-of-office-politics [accessed 1 May 2025].

10. Richards, L., 'Office Politics: How to Handle It', *Intelligent People*.

11. Collins, J., *Good to Great: Why Some Companies Make the Leap and Others Don't* (New York: Harper Business, 2001).

12. Niccolò Machiavelli, *Discourses on Livy,* trans. Harvey C. Mansfield and Nathan Tarcov. (Chicago, University of Chicago Press, 1996).

13. Smith, J., *Good Self, Bad Self* (New York: Free Press, 2013).

14. Kellerman, B. *Bad leadership: What it is, how it happens, why it matters.* Boston, MA: Harvard Business School Press, 2004.

15. McCray, V., *How to Swim with the Sharks: A Survival Guide for Leadership in Diverse Environments* (Charleston, SC: CreateSpace, 2014).

16. Ibid.

17. Billan, R., 'How to Overcome Tall Poppy Syndrome and Create a Culture of Inclusivity', *The Future Economy* (2023), available at: https://thefutureeconomy.ca/op-eds/tall-poppy-syndrome-rumeet-billan-women-of-influence/ [accessed 28 February 2023].

Chapter 6

1. Li, K., Mai, F., Shen, R., Yang, C. and Zhang, T., 'Dissecting Corporate Culture Using Generative AI – Insights from Analyst Reports', *ECGI Global* (2024), available at: https://www.ecgi.global/sites/default/files/Paper%3A%20 Dissecting%20Corporate%20Culture%20Using%20 Generative%20AI%20%20%E2%80%93%20Insights%20 from%20Analyst%20Reports.pdf [accessed 6 May 2025].

2. Della Cava, M., 'Microsoft's Satya Nadella Is Counting on Culture Shock to Drive Growth', USA Today (2017), available at: https://eu.usatoday.com/story/tech/ news/2017/02/20/microsofts-satya-nadella-counting-culture- shock-drive-growth/98011388/ [accessed 6 May 2024].

3. Ibid.

4. Ibid.

5. Wikipedia, 'Satya Nadella', *Wikipedia: The Free Encyclopedia*, available at: https://en.wikipedia.org/wiki/Satya_Nadella [accessed 6 May 2025].

6. Schein, E.H. and Schein, P.A., *Organisational Culture and Leadership*, 5th edn (Hoboken, NJ: Wiley, 2017).

7. Hall, E.T., *Beyond Culture* (New York: Anchor Books, 1976).

8. Patel, K., 'Top 11 Failed Mergers and Acquisitions of All Time', *M&A Science* (n.d.), available at: https://www. mascience.com/community-blog/top-11-failed-mergers-

and-acquisitions-of-all-time#:~:text=In%202007%2C%20
Daimler%20Benz%20sold,famous%20M%26A%20fails%20
in%20history. [accessed 6 May 2025].

9. Li et al., 'Dissecting Corporate Culture Using Generative AI.'

10. Egan, G. (1994). *Working the shadow side: A guide to positive behind-the-scenes management.* San Francisco, CA: Jossey-Bass.

11. Padilla, A., Hogan, R. and Kaiser, R.B., 'The Toxic Triangle: Destructive Leaders, Susceptible Followers, and Conducive Environments', *The Leadership Quarterly*, 18 (2007), pp. 176–194.

12. Li et al., 'Dissecting Corporate Culture Using Generative AI.'

13. Newton, R., 'Retaining the Best of Your Culture Amid Organisational Change', *Harvard Business Review* (2023), available at: https://hbr.org/2023/11/retaining-the-best-of-your-culture-amid-organizational-change [accessed 29 February 2024].

Chapter 7

1. Van Vugt, M. (2006) "The Evolutionary Origins of Leadership and Followership", University of Kent at Canterbury. Available online https://www.professormarkvanvugt.com/images/files/TheEvolutionaryOriginsofLeadershipandFollowership-2003.pdf, as at 23.04.25.

2. Ibid.

3. Ibid.

4. Llopis, G., '8 Reasons Leadership Is Hard and Why Few Are Prepared to Lead', *Forbes* (2025), available at: https://www.forbes.com/sites/glennllopis/2025/05/05/8-reasons-leadership-is-hard-and-why-few-are-prepared-to-lead/ [accessed 13 May 2025].

5. Rizvi, J., 'Transformative Leadership: The Art of Inspiring Leaders Around You', *Forbes* (2024), available at: https://www.forbes.com/sites/jiawertz/2024/01/20/transformative-leadership-the-art-of-inspiring-leaders-around-you/amp/ [accessed 28 February 2024].

About the Author

Heather Connery (BA, MBA, CMgr FCMI, FRAI, FRSA, MTAA) is a Cultural Anthropologist and leadership expert. A multidisciplinary leader, coach, and author, she has built a portfolio career spanning consultancy, business ownership, board-level advisory, research, writing and social impact. She has worked with organisations from global corporates to start-ups and non-profits, specialising in decoding the real dynamics of leadership and culture to help individuals and organisations navigate complexity with clarity, influence and sustainable impact.

Heather is the Founder and Managing Director of three businesses: U-G-U, a bespoke coaching practice for emerging and experienced leaders; AnthrOrg, which applies cultural anthropology to strategic business challenges; and WisN, focused on holistic wellbeing. Her corporate career includes senior roles such as Chief of Staff, Head of Strategic Projects & Innovation and Head of Risk & Transformation Management Office, where she led large-scale transformation, governance excellence, and cultural change initiatives.

An MBA graduate with Distinction, Heather holds Fellowships with the Chartered Management Institute, the Royal Anthropological

Institute and the Royal Society of Arts, Manufacturing and Commerce. She is also a certified therapist, accredited coach, and award-winning mentor, having supported hundreds of professionals to grow their influence, navigate organisational politics, and achieve meaningful success.

After more than two decades moving between worlds – from boardrooms to the shop floor – Heather has learned that leadership is rarely just about strategy or skill. It's about navigating the unspoken codes that shape how people behave, decide, and lead. Her mission is to help others see those rules clearly and provide them with the tools to navigate without losing their way. For her, leadership is about creating the conditions for people and organisations to thrive, shaping optimal cultures, and ensuring the way results are achieved matters as much as the results themselves.

Through her platforms, Leadership Decoded and Leadership Code Breaker, Heather combines governance excellence, psychology, anthropology and her own lived experience to challenge conventional leadership narratives and unlock human potential.

Heather lives in the UK with her husband, children, and what she fondly calls "the zoo" — a lively mix of much-loved animals.

If you'd like to continue the conversation and/or work with Heather, you can connect via:

> LinkedIn: www.linkedin.com/in/heather-connery
> Email: heather.connery@u-g-u.co.uk
> Instagram: instagram.com/leadercodebreaker

For the online resources mentioned in this book, visit u-g-u.co.uk/membership-page.

Bibliography

Aabo, T., Pantzalis, C., Park, J.C., Trigeorgis, L. and Wulff, J.N., 'CEO Personality Traits, Strategic Flexibility, and Firm Dynamics', *Journal of Corporate Finance*, 84 (2024), 102524.

Alvesson, M. and Sveningsson, S., 'Managers Doing Leadership: The Extra-Ordinarization of the Mundane', *Human Relations*, 56 (2003), pp. 1435–1459.

Babiak, P. and Hare, R.D., *Snakes in Suits: When Psychopaths Go to Work* (New York: HarperCollins, 2007).

Blake, R.R., & Mouton, J.S. (1964). *The Managerial Grid: The Key to Leadership Excellence*. Houston, Gulf Publishing Company.

Cambridge Dictionary, 'Leader', available at: https://dictionary.cambridge.org/dictionary/english/leader [accessed 28 February 2023].

Carnegie, D., *How to Win Friends and Influence People* (Wilco Publishing House, 2017 edn; originally published 1936).

Castrillon, C., '5 Powerful Strategies to Build Trust in the Workplace', *Forbes* (2023), available at: https://www.forbes.com/sites/carolinecastrillon/2023/12/17/5-powerful-ways-to-build-trust-in-the-workplace/?sh=627f6c693817 [accessed 28 February 2023].

Cecchi-Dimeglio, P., 'Steps for Creating a Successful Leadership Development Plan', *Forbes* (2024), available at: https://www.forbes.com/sites/paolacecchi-dimeglio/2024/01/04/five-steps-for-creating-a-successful-leadership-development-plan/amp/ [accessed 28 February 2024].

Cohen, E.G., 'The Fear of Losing Control', *Psychology Today* (2011), available at: https://www.psychologytoday.com/gb/blog/what-would-aristotle-do/201105/the-fear-losing-control [accessed 28 February 2011].

Corbett, J., 'Where Do Leaders Come From?', *Developmental Leadership Program, University of Birmingham* (2019), available at: https://dlprog.org/publications/foundational-papers/where-do-leaders-come-from/ [accessed 22 April 2024].

Danyal, A., 'The Fine Line Between Confidence and Arrogance', *Leadership Right* (2024), available at: https://www.leadershipright.com/p/the-fine-line-between-confidence-and-arrogance [accessed 29 February 2024].

Egan, G. (1994). *Working the shadow side: A guide to positive behind-the-scenes management.* San Francisco, CA: Jossey-Bass.

Ericsson, K.A., Krampe, R.T. and Tesch-Römer, C., 'The Role of Deliberate Practice in the Acquisition of Expert Performance', *Psychological Review*, 100.3 (1993), pp. 363–406.

Farnham, D., *Human Resource Management in Context*, 4th edn (London: CIPD, 2015), pp. 190–195.

Finkelstein, S., 'What Amazing Bosses Do Differently', *Harvard Business Review* (2015), available at: https://hbr.org/2015/11/what-amazing-bosses-do-differently [accessed 29 February 2024].

Four Day Week Global, 'The 4 Day Week UK Results' (2025), available at: https://www.4dayweek.com/uk-pilot-results [accessed 30 April 2025].

Gallup, *State of the Global Workplace* (2025), available at: https://www.gallup.com/workplace/349484/state-of-the-global-workplace.aspx [accessed 1 May 2025].

Gleeson, B., 'The Leadership Dichotomy of Ego and Humility', *Forbes* (2024), available at: https://www.forbes.com/sites/brentgleeson/2024/04/05/the-leadership-dichotomy-of-ego-and-humility/ [accessed 8 May 2025].

Greene, R., *The 48 Laws of Power* (London: Profile Books, 2002).

Hewlett, S.A. and Buck Luce, C., 'Extreme Jobs: The Dangerous Allure of the 70-Hour Workweek', *Harvard Business Review* (2006), available at: https://hbr.org/2006/12/extreme-jobs-the-dangerous-allure-of-the-70-hour-workweek [accessed 30 April 2025].

Johnson, S., *Who Moved My Cheese?* (London: Vermilion, 1998).

Keller, S., 'Attracting and Retaining the Right Talent', *McKinsey & Company* (2017), available at: https://www.mckinsey.com/capabilities/people-and-organizational-performance/our-insights/attracting-and-retaining-the-right-talent#/ [accessed 15 April 2025].

Keller, S., 'High-Performing Teams: A Timeless Leadership Topic', *McKinsey & Company* (2017), available at: https://www.mckinsey.com/capabilities/people-and-organizational-performance/our-insights/high-performing-teams-a-timeless-leadership-topic#/ [accessed 30 April 2025].

Kellerman, B. (2004). *Bad leadership: What it is, how it happens, why it matters*. Boston, MA: Harvard Business School Press.

Knight, R., '8 Essential Qualities of Successful Leaders', *Harvard Business Review* (2023), available at: https://hbr.org/2023/12/8-essential-qualities-of-successful-leaders [accessed 23 April 2025].

Laker, B., 'Leading with Vision: The Delicate Dance of Assertiveness', *Forbes* (2023), available at: https://www.forbes.com/sites/benjaminlaker/2023/12/08/leading-with-vision-the-delicate-dance-of-assertiveness/?sh=7c58705f161b [accessed 29 February 2024].

Laker, B., 'Quick Choices, Lasting Impact: The Risks of Quick Leadership Decisions', *Forbes* (2023), available at: https://www.forbes.com/sites/benjaminlaker/2023/12/05/quick-choices-lasting-impact-the-risks-of-quick-leadership-decisions/?sh=a835f881ddb9 [accessed 29 February 2024].

Leonhard, G., *Digital Transformation: Are You Ready for Exponential Change?* (2016), available at: https://www.youtube.com/watch?v=ystdF6jN7hc [accessed 14 April 2025].

Llopis, G., '8 Reasons Leadership Is Hard and Why Few Are Prepared to Lead', *Forbes* (2025), available at: https://www.forbes.com/sites/glennllopis/2025/05/05/8-reasons-leadership-is-hard-and-why-few-are-prepared-to-lead/ [accessed 13 May 2025].

Marr, B., 'Cultural Intelligence (CQ) Is an Important Predictor of Success. Here's How to Boost Your CQ', *Forbes* (2022), available at: https://www.forbes.com/sites/bernardmarr/2022/09/05/cultural-intelligence-cq-is-an-important-predictor-of-success-heres-how-to-boost-your-cq/ [accessed 22 April 2025].

Meyer, C., 'Tall Poppy Syndrome in the Workplace and the Laws of Power', *The Mind Collection* (n.d.), available at: https://themindcollection.com/tall-poppy-syndrome/ [accessed 29 February 2024].

Moore, K., 'How Leaders Can Shape Organisational Change, BCG Study Reveals', *Forbes* (2023), available at: https://www.forbes.com/sites/karlmoore/2023/12/12/how-leaders-can-shape-organizational-change-bcg-study-reveals/?sh=4af8de9214ec [accessed 29 February 2024].

Moore, M.G., 'You're a Leader Now. Not Everyone Is Going to Like You', *Harvard Business Review* (2021), available at: https://hbr.org/2021/09/youre-a-leader-now-not-everyone-is-going-to-like-you [accessed 28 February 2024].

Neal, L., 'Empowering Women to Overcome Tall Poppy Syndrome and Advance Inclusion', *We Are The City* (2023), available at: https://wearethecity.com/empowering-women-to-overcome-tall-poppy-syndrome-and-advance-inclusion/ [accessed 28 February 2024].

Neal, S., Rhyne, R., Paese, M.J., Watt, B. and Yeh, M., *CEO Leadership Report 2023* (2023), available at: https://www.ddiworld.com/glf/ceo-leadership-report-2023 [accessed 28 February 2024].

Nohria, N., 'Leaders Must React', *Harvard Business Review* (2024), available at: https://hbr.org/2024/01/leaders-must-react [accessed 29 February 2024].

Pfeffer, J., *Leadership BS: Fixing Workplaces and Careers One Truth at a Time* (New York: HarperCollins, 2015).

Phipps, M. and Gautrey, C., *21 Dirty Tricks at Work: How to Beat the Game of Office Politics* (Chichester: Capstone Publishing, 2005).

Quinn, R., Crane, B., Thompson, T. and Quinn, R.E., 'Why Real-Time Leadership Is So Hard', *Harvard Business Review* (2024), available at: https://hbr.org/2024/01/why-real-time-leadership-is-so-hard [accessed 29 February 2024].

Richards, L., 'Office Politics: How to Handle It', *Intelligent People* (2024), available at: https://www.intelligentpeople.co.uk/employer-advice/office-politics/ [accessed 1 May 2025].

Robinson, B., '4 Strategies to Avoid the Hazards of "Ivory Tower Syndrome" in Remote Work', *Forbes* (2023), available at: https://

www.forbes.com/sites/bryanrobinson/2023/11/13/4-strategies-to-avoid-the-hazards-of-ivory-tower-syndrome-in-remote-work/?sh=633212ef2918 [accessed 29 February 2024].

Ruscio, J. and Amabile, T.M., 'How Does Creativity Happen?', *Harvard Business School* (1996).

Schein, E.H. and Schein, P.A., *Humble Leadership* (Oakland, CA: Berrett-Koehler Publishers, 2023).

Schwantes, M., '4 Big Reasons Why Your CEO Is Not Executing as a Leader', *Inc.* (2023), available at: https://www.inc.com/marcel-schwantes/4-big-reasons-why-your-ceo-is-not-executing-as-a-leader.html [accessed 28 February 2024].

Schwantes, M., 'Elon Musk Says What Separates Great Leaders from the Pack Comes Down to 3 Words', *Inc.* (2023), available at: https://www.inc.com/marcel-schwantes/elon-musk-says-what-separates-great-leaders-from-pack-really-comes-down-to-3-words.html [accessed 29 February 2024].

Spencer Stuart, *UK Spencer Stuart Board Index* (2024), available at: https://www.spencerstuart.com/research-and-insight/uk-board-index/the-board [accessed 14 April 2025].

Spillane, J.P., *Distributed Leadership* (San Francisco: Jossey-Bass, 2006).

Vinkenburg, C.J., van Engen, M.L., Eagly, A.H. and Johannesen-Schmidt, M.C., 'An Exploration of Stereotypical Beliefs about

Leadership Styles: Is Transformational Leadership a Route to Women's Promotion?', *The Leadership Quarterly*, 22 (2011), pp. 10–21.

Wakeman, C., *Reality-Based Leadership* (San Francisco: Jossey-Bass, 2010).

Wells, R., '10 Leadership Quotes for Leaders and Managers in 2024', *Forbes* (2024), available at: https://www.forbes.com/sites/rachelwells/2024/01/25/10-leadership-quotes-for-leaders-and-managers-in-2024/?sh=6e6cc8997122 [accessed 29 February 2024].

Wiessner, D., 'Tesla Must Face Class Action Claims by 6,000 US Workers in Race Bias Case', *Reuters* (2024), available at: https://www.reuters.com/legal/tesla-must-face-class-action-claims-by-6000-workers-race-bias-case-2024-02-29/ [accessed 29 February 2024].

Wikipedia, 'Cultural Intelligence', *Wikipedia: The Free Encyclopedia*, available at: https://en.wikipedia.org/wiki/Cultural_intelligence [accessed 29 February 2024].

Wikipedia, 'Leadership', *Wikipedia: The Free Encyclopedia*, available at: https://en.wikipedia.org/wiki/Leadership [accessed 29 February 2024].

Wikipedia, 'Psychopathy in the Workplace', *Wikipedia: The Free Encyclopedia*, available at: https://en.wikipedia.org/wiki/Psychopathy_in_the_workplace [accessed 29 February 2024].

CIO.de, '7 Thesen zum Digitalen Führen', available at: https://www.cio.de/article/3690825/7-thesen-zum-digitalen-fuehren.html [accessed 29 February 2024].

Wikipedia, 'Who Moved My Cheese?', *Wikipedia: The Free Encyclopedia*, available at: https://en.wikipedia.org/wiki/Who_Moved_My_Cheese%3F [accessed 29 February 2024].

Williams, R., 'When Your CEO Is a Psychopath', *Medium* (2023), available at: https://raybwilliams.medium.com/when-your-ceo-is-a-psychopath-f4e3caf1fbf4 [accessed 14 April 2025].

Zaleznik, A., 'Power and Politics in Organisational Life', *Harvard Business Review* (1970), available at: https://hbr.org/1970/05/power-and-politics-in-organizational-life [accessed 28 February 2024].

www.ingramcontent.com/pod-product-compliance
Lightning Source LLC
Chambersburg PA
CBHW071206210326
41597CB00016B/1697